rice & noodle

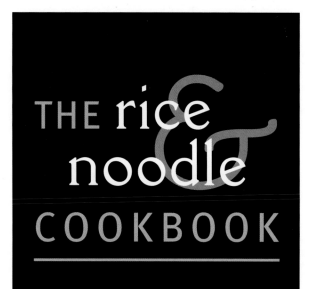

THE rice & noodle COOKBOOK

100 delicious
step-by-step recipes

Consulting editors:
Christine Ingram and Roz Denny

LORENZ BOOKS

First published in 1999 by Lorenz Books

LORENZ BOOKS are available for bulk purchase for sales promotion and for premium use. For details, write or call the sales director, Lorenz Books, 27 West 20th Street, New York, NY 10011; (800) 354-9657

Lorenz Books is an imprint of Anness Publishing Inc.

ISBN 0 7548 0158 6

Publisher: Joanna Lorenz
Senior Cookery Editor: Linda Fraser
Project Editors: Zoe Antoniou, Margaret Malone and Emma Clegg
Designers: Joyce Chester and Lilian Lindblom
Jacket Designer: Luise Roberts
Photographers: Karl Adamson, Edward Allwright, David Armstrong, Steve Baxter, James Duncan, Michelle Garrett, Amanda Heywood, Tim Hill, Janine Hosegood, David Jordan, Don Last, William Lingwood, Patrick McLeavey, Michael Michaels, Thomas Odulate and Juliet Piddington.
Recipes: Alex Barker, Carla Capalbo, Kit Chan, Frances Cleary, Roz Denny, Matthew Drennan, Sarah Edmonds, Rafi Fernandez, Christine France, Silvana Franco, Sarah Gates, Shirley Gill, Rosamund Grant, Janine Hosegood, Deh-Ta Hsiung, Shehzad Husain, Peter Jordan, Manisha Kanani, Soheila Kimberley, Masaki Ko, Ruby Le Bois, Patricia Lousada, Lesley Mackley, Norma MacMillan, Sue Maggs, Sarah Maxwell, Sallie Morris, Janice Murfitt, Angela Nilsen, Elisabeth Lambert Ortiz, Maggie Pannell, Anne Sheasby, Liz Trigg, Hilaire Walden, Laura Washburn, Steven Wheeler and Elizabeth Wolf-Cohen.
Stylists: Madeleine Brehaut, Clare Hunt, Maria Kelly, Marion McLornan, Blake Minton, Marion Price and Elizabeth Wolf-Cohen.
Food for photography: Jacqueline Clark, Joanne Craig, Katherine Hawkins, Jane Stevenson, Carol Tennant and Judy Williams.

Previously published as two separate titles:
50 Delicious Noodle Dishes and *50 Classic Rice Recipes*

Printed and bound in Hong Kong/China

1 2 3 4 5 6 7 8 9 10

contents

rice 6

noodles 98

rice

Introducing Rice

Rice is central to many of the world's greatest cuisines and can be used in a host of ways, both savory and sweet. No other food is quite this versatile. In the West, we have just begun to appreciate the great potential of this glorious grain, and instead of relegating it to the side of our plates as an accompaniment, we now look upon rice as the basis of a delicious meal.

Around two-thirds of the world's population are nourished every day on rice. There are thought to be about 7,000 varieties of rice grown across the globe, all with different qualities and characteristics. Rice is highly recommended by doctors and nutritionists, as it is high in carbohydrates and low in fat, making it a healthy source of energy that is also easily digestible.

Rice was one of the first cereals to be cultivated thousands of years ago from a variety of wild grasses in many different parts of Asia. There was no one specific birthplace. The numerous varieties common today in rice-eating countries evolved according to the climate and terrain and the developing agricultural practices of the time. Even today, many new strains of rice continue to be developed.

The main rice-growing regions of the world are China, Japan, India, Indonesia, Thailand, the southern states of the US and areas of Spain and Italy. The great joy of rice cooking is the incredible variety of dishes one can make. There are the shaped sushi of Japan, the pressed rice cakes of Thailand, pilafs of India and the Middle East, risottos and paellas of the Mediterranean, jambalayas of America and rice and peas of the West Indies—the list can be endless and the variety inspirational.

Types of Rice

Rice is selected for a dish according to the length of the grain. There are two main categories of rice, long- and short-grain.

Long-Grain Rices

Long-grain rices (*Oryza indica*) contain high levels of amylase starch, which keeps the grains more separate after cooking. They are excellent steamed or baked, in pilafs and salads. Long-grain rices are also known collectively as Patna rices, because much of the long-grain rice sold to Europe originally came from around the city of Patna in India.

Basmati Rice

This long-grain rice is highly aromatic—its name means "fragrant" in Hindi. It is ideal for delicate pilafs. Basmati rice benefits from being rinsed in a bowl with plenty of cold water and soaked for 30 minutes before cooking to lighten the grain.

Brown Rice

This long-grain rice has only its outer husk removed, leaving a nutritious bran layer. It is therefore higher in fiber and has a slightly nutty taste and chewy texture. This rice can take up to 40 minutes to cook; more water will be required to allow for this longer cooking time. Brown (and white) long-grain rice is available in par-boiled, or converted, versions, which means that it has been heat-treated with high-pressure steam, making it nonstick. This does, however, remove much of the natural flavor, and the rice can take longer to cook and has an even chewier texture. Brown basmati is lighter than other brown grains; it takes about 25 minutes to cook.

Red Rices

In the wild, rice is actually a light red color. Sometimes this characteristic is bred back into long-grain rices. Examples of these rices are Wehani rice from California and, more recently, a semiwild cultivated red rice from the Camargue in France, similar to buckwheat in flavor.

Thai Rices

Thai fragrant or Thai jasmine are high-quality long-grain rices that have a slight stickiness to them and a delicate fragrance. They take even less time to cook than basmati and are best cooked by the covered pan/absorption method with one and a quarter times the volume of water to rice. No salt is added during cooking.

White Rice

This is the most widely used long-grain rice and is mild in flavor. Long-grain rice grown in the United States and often exported to Europe is of excellent quality, especially rice from Arkansas, Texas and California.

Wild Rice

This is not actually a true rice at all but a form of aquatic grass found growing around lakes in Canada and the United States. The best type of wild rice is long, dark brown and glossy. The grains should be cooked until they burst open, releasing their natural deliciously nutty aroma. They take up to 50 minutes to cook, and need to be well submerged in water for most of that time. A form of smaller-grain, cultivated wild rice is more readily available and cheaper. It can sometimes also be found in a blend with converted long–grains.

Short-Grain Rices

Short-grain rice (*Oryza japonica*), or round-grain, is high in amylopectin, which gives a starchy quality so that the grains cling together after cooking. Short-grain rice is often used to make rice pudding, because the grains absorb much liquid to make a creamy, rich texture that is essential to the dish. Short-grain rice can also be used for risotto, croquettes, sushi and some stir-fried dishes.

Glutinous Rices

These are stickier than Thai rices. The name is misleading, since the grains contain no gluten. These rices are ideal for sushi, as the rice sticks together for shaping and rolling. Japanese rice is a short-grain glutinous rice, easy to pick up and dip into sauces. Glutinous rices can be black or white and are often used for desserts served with sugar and coconut cream.

Risotto Rices

These short-grain rices have high levels of starch. Good risotto rice gives a nice creaminess to a dish, yet the grain still retains an al dente bite. Some of the best risotto rices are carnaroli, arborio and Vialone Nano. Stock is added gradually when making risotto, but if making paella with this grain, add the stock all at once and simmer without stirring.

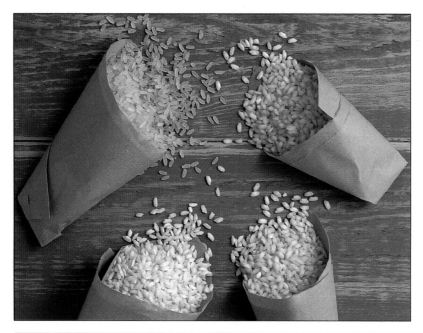

Left (clockwise from top left): Arborio and three varieties of carnaroli rices. Opposite: Brown, long-grain, converted, brown basmati, basmati and American long-grain rices (center).

Equipment

The list of equipment that is useful in a kitchen is endless. Some utensils are particularly handy for preparing rice, and will make cooking your favorite dishes much easier.

Colander
This is essential for draining the water from rice when it has been rinsed or boiled. Use a colander with small holes.

Food Processor
The food processor is useful for mixing and blending ingredients. Most have an attachment for slicing and grating large quantities, which helps to prepare ingredients more quickly, especially since some rice does not take a long time to cook.

Fork
Use a fork to simply fluff up the grains of cooked rice.

Frying Pan
This is useful for sautéed rice. Frying pans are also useful if you are preparing stir-fry recipes when a wok is unavailable.

Measuring Cups and Spoons
Measuring cups and spoons are useful for gauging accurately the volume of ingredients. Spoon measures range from $\frac{1}{8}$ teaspoon to 1 tablespoon and cups from $\frac{1}{8}$ cup to 1 cup.

Mixing Bowls
Glass mixing bowls that fit neatly inside each other are useful for a number of recipe preparations, such as making rice salads or mixing desserts.

Mortar and Pestle
This is useful for grinding small amounts of spices, and it is worth buying one if you enjoy cooking with fresh spices regularly.

Rice Cooker
Rice cookers are very useful and make a good investment if you cook rice regularly. They can produce good results with rice, and will free the stove for cooking other ingredients. They are more suitable for cooking sticky and converted grains than basmati rice, which needs to be parboiled first. A rice cooker will also keep rice warm for up to five hours. Leftover rice can be reheated the following day, and the cooker can also be used for steaming many other dishes.

Rice Paddle
This is an ideal utensil for serving cooked rice.

Saucepan
A good stainless-steel saucepan with a tight-fitting lid is essential for cooking rice properly. It is a sound investment for any cook. The best pans tend to be sold individually rather than as a set. They are expensive but will last a lifetime of simmering and boiling.

Steamers
Steamers are used for cooking sticky rice or sticky-rice balls. When these small items are being cooked, line the baskets with pieces of rinsed cheesecloth. Bamboo, stacking-type steamers are available in many sizes from a wide range of stores. When not in use, they look very attractive on a shelf in the kitchen. Like almost all utensils in the Asian kitchen, they are multipurpose. Indeed, the baskets can be used for serving as well as cooking foods.

Whisk
A sturdy whisk is useful for beating eggs, combining ingredients such as salad dressings and for mixing sauces to a smooth consistency. The best ones are made of stainless steel.

Wok
The wok is ideal for stir-frying a number of rice dishes. There are several varieties available, including the carbon-steel round-bottomed wok, or Pau wok. This is best suited to a gas stove, where you will be able to control the amount of heat needed more easily. The carbon-steel flat-bottomed wok is best for use on electric or solid-fuel stoves, as it will give a better distribution of heat. One useful cooking tip is to warm the wok gently before adding the oil for cooking. The oil then floods easily over the surface of the pan and prevents the food from sticking. Less oil is required when using a wok than in conventional pans.

Right: A selection of some of the most common and useful kitchen utensils.

Plain Long-Grain Rice

Use white long-grain rice throughout, unless otherwise specified. Remember to adjust your cooking method if using a different grain.

The Open Pan/Fast Boiling Method

This is the simplest method. The rice is cooked in a large amount of boiling water over medium heat until al dente. It is then drained and rinsed. Long-grain white rice will take about 15 minutes to cook, and brown rice 30-35 minutes. If using converted rice, follow the directions on the package.

The Covered Pan/Absorption Method

In this method (shown here), the rice is steamed. It simmers gently in a measured amount of water in a covered saucepan until all the water has been absorbed. This has the added bonus of retaining valuable nutrients that would be discarded with the water if the rice was boiled.

Serves 4

INGREDIENTS
1⅓ cups white long-grain rice
pinch of salt

COOK'S TIP
Precisely how much liquid to use, and the cooking time, will vary depending on the type of rice used, the width of the saucepan (and how snugly its lid fits) and the heat of the stove. For 1⅓ cups brown rice, use 2½ cups water and cook for 25-35 minutes.

1 Wash the rice in several changes of cold water to remove excess starch, and drain. This is important, because the rice is not rinsed at the end as it is with the boiling method. Place the rice in a saucepan and add 2 cups cold water. (There should be no more than about ⅔ inch of water above the surface of the rice.)

2 Bring to a boil and add the salt, then stir to prevent the rice from sticking to the bottom of the pan. Reduce the heat to very, very low, cover the pan tightly and cook for 15–20 minutes, or until all the water has been absorbed.

3 Remove from the heat and let stand with the lid on for 5–10 minutes. Fluff up the rice with a fork or spoon just before serving. Rice cooked by the boiling method should also be fluffed up before being served.

VARIATIONS

There are a number of other ways to cook rice. These are more commonly used when rice is cooked with other ingredients in a recipe, such as a stir-fry or casserole. Follow the instructions below to sauté or bake rice. See the Covered Pan/Absorption Method (opposite) for quantities and timings, but use boiling rather than cold water. You may need more water when cooking by the sauté method.

Rice for Salads

This recipe uses cooked rice. Try to cook rice freshly for a salad rather than use leftover cold rice, as the result is much better. This is a basic recipe for a rice salad, but you can add a variety of ingredients.

Serves 4

INGREDIENTS
scant 1 cup long-grain rice, cooked
5 tablespoons selected vinaigrette
1/2 cup black olives
1/2 cup chopped scallionss
1/2 cup chopped celery
1/2 cup chopped radishes
1/2 cup chopped cucumber
salt and freshly ground black pepper
parsley sprigs, to garnish

1 Place the cooked, rinsed and drained rice in a bowl and add the vinaigrette of your choice, together with seasoning. Let the mixture stand for a good 15 minutes. This method ensures a delicious, light salad where the dressing has been absorbed into the grain instead of a more cloying dressing that simply coats the sides.

2 Quarter the olives, discarding the pits, and add to the rice with the other ingredients. Toss well and garnish with sprigs of parsley.

1 ▲To sauté rice, heat a small amount of oil, butter, or a mixture of the two in a saucepan over medium heat. Add the rice and stir to coat the grains. Sauté for 2–3 minutes, stirring constantly.

2 Add the measured quantity of boiling salted water. Bring back to a boil, then cover and steam over very low heat until all the water has been absorbed and the rice is tender.

1 ▲To bake rice, preheat the oven to 350°F. Place the washed and rinsed rice in a baking dish and add the measured boiling salted water.

2 Cover tightly with foil or a lid and bake until the water has been absorbed and the rice is tender; 20-30 minutes for white rice and 35-40 for brown. Cooking time depends on many factors, including how tightly covered the dish is.

REHEATING RICE

Always reheat cooked rice thorougly for at least 5 minutes, until it is piping hot, especially if stir-frying. This is very important, as cooked rice can harbor spores of bacteria. If rice is reheated on several occasions, or kept warm for a long time, the bacteria may germinate and multiply. Food poisoning could result.

STORING RICE

Cooked leftover rice can be stored for up to 2 days in the refrigerator. Rice can be frozen, but this affects the starch granules, making the rice seem chalky when reheated.

Basmati Rice

In India, basmati rice is consumed in great quantities by all members of society. Using ghee instead of butter or oil produces an authentic flavor.

Serves 4

INGREDIENTS
¾ teaspoon ghee, unsalted butter or olive oil
1⅓ cups basmati rice, washed and drained
salt, to taste

1 Heat the ghee, butter or oil in a saucepan and sauté the drained rice thoroughly for 2–3 minutes.

2 Add 2 cups of water and salt and bring to a boil. Reduce the heat to low, cover and cook gently for 15–20 minutes, until all the water is absorbed. Let stand, covered, for 5 minutes. Fluff the grains before serving.

Jasmine Rice

A naturally aromatic long-grain white rice, jasmine rice is a staple of most Thai meals. Salt is not added to this delicate rice during cooking.

Serves 4

INGREDIENTS
1¾ cups jasmine rice

1 Rinse the rice thoroughly in cold water until the water runs clear. Place the rice in a heavy saucepan and add 2½ cups cold water. Bring to a vigorous boil, uncovered, over high heat.

2 Stir and reduce the heat to low. Cover and simmer for 12–15 minutes, or until all the water has been absorbed. Remove from the heat and let stand for 10 minutes. Fluff up and separate the grains with a fork.

Wild Rice

This aquatic grass is deliciously nutty and firm. It is cooked in the same way as long-grain rice, but needs a longer cooking time.

Serves 4

INGREDIENTS
pinch of salt
generous 1 cup wild rice

1 Place 4 cups cold water in a saucepan and add the salt. Bring to a boil.

2 ▲ Add the rice to the saucepan and bring back to a boil. Cook the rice for 45–50 minutes. The rice is ready when it has become tender but still firm and the grains have begun to split open. Drain well and serve.

COOK'S TIP
Wild rice perfectly complements meat and poultry dishes. It is also an excellent partner for vegetables such as winter squashes and mushrooms.

Glutinous Rice

The term glutinous is a little misleading, as the rice does not actually contain gluten. It is also known as sticky rice and can be black as well as white.

Serves 4

INGREDIENTS
$2^2/_3$ cups glutinous (sticky) rice
1 teaspoon vegetable oil
$^1/_2$ teaspoon salt

1 Rinse the rice in cold water until it runs clear. Place in a bowl with plenty of water and let soak for 1 hour.

2 ▲ Drain, pour into a bowl and add the oil and salt. Line a large steamer with a piece of clean cheesecloth. Transfer the rice to the steamer. Steam over boiling water for about 45 minutes, stirring from time to time.

COOK'S TIP
Glutinous rice is often served as a dessert, particularly in Thailand. It can be accompanied simply with sugar and coconut cream.

Risotto Rice

This short-grain rice absorbs cooking liquid and becomes beautifully creamy. A risotto can be served as a first course, a main dish or an accompaniment. This recipe is basic but flavorful. The garlic can be omitted.

Serves 4

INGREDIENTS
5½ cups chicken stock
2 tablespoons butter or oil
½ onion, chopped
2 garlic cloves, crushed (optional)
1¾ cups risotto rice

risotto rice   *oil*   *onion*   *garlic*   *chicken stock*

1   In a saucepan, bring the stock to a boil, then reduce the heat so that the liquid is kept at a gentle simmer.

2   Heat the butter or oil, or a mixture of the two, in a wide, heavy saucepan. Add the chopped onion and crushed garlic, if using, and cook over low heat until soft, stirring occasionally.

3   Add the rice and stir to coat it with the fat. Sauté for 1–2 minutes over moderate heat, stirring.

4   Add a little of the simmering stock (about a ladleful) and stir well. Simmer, stirring frequently, until the rice has absorbed almost all the liquid.

5   Add a little more of the simmering stock and cook, stirring, until it is almost all absorbed. Continue adding the stock in this way until the grains of rice are tender but still firm to the bite, or al dente, and the risotto is creamy but not runny. You may not need to add all the stock. Total cooking time will be about 30 minutes.

COOK'S TIP

You can use arborio rice for risottos throughout, if you like, as it is a good medium-grain risotto rice, while superfine arborio rice is one of the best. This swells to at least three times its original size during cooking, enabling the rice to absorb all the cooking liquid for a creamy, smooth texture <u>while still</u> retaining the shape of the grains.

Japanese Rice for Sushi

The Japanese prefer their rice slightly sticky so it can be easily eaten with chopsticks, shaped into rice balls or used to make sushi. Use Japanese rice if you can find it; otherwise substitute Thai or long-grain rice.

Serves 4

INGREDIENTS
1³/₄ cups Japanese rice, washed and
  drained
1 piece kombu, 2 inches square
  (optional)

MIXED VINEGAR
3 tablespoons rice vinegar or distilled
  white vinegar
3 tablespoons sugar
2 teaspoons sea salt

kombu

*Japanese
rice*

salt

sugar

*rice
vinegar*

1 Place the rice in a large, heavy saucepan, cover with 5 cups boiling water and add the kombu, if using. Stir once and simmer, uncovered, for 15 minutes. Turn off the heat, cover and let stand for another 5 minutes to allow the rice to finish cooking in its own steam. Before serving, the rice should be fluffed with chopsticks or a fork. This rice is a Japanese staple.

COOK'S TIP

The washing process for Japanese rice is very important, as it improves the flavor of the cooked rice. It must be washed several times in cold water until the water runs clear. Thai or long-grain rice should only be washed once for sushi recipes, so that the grains become slightly sticky when cooked. Note that cooked Japanese rice should not be stored in the refrigerator, because it will harden.

2 To prepare sushi rice, make the dressing by heating the vinegar in a small saucepan, with a lid to keep in the strong vapors. Add the sugar and salt and dissolve. Allow to cool. Spread the cooked rice out on a bamboo mat or tray and allow to cool.

3 Pour on the dressing and fluff with chopsticks or a fork. Keep covered until ready to use.

Beef and Rice Soup

This classic Iranian soup, *aashe maste*, is extremely substantial and almost makes a meal in itself. It is full of invigorating herbs and is a popular cold-weather dish.

Serves 6

INGREDIENTS
2 large onions
2 tablespoons oil
1 tablespoon ground turmeric
½ cup yellow split peas
8 ounces ground beef
1 cup long-grain rice
3 tablespoons each chopped fresh
    parsley, cilantro and chives
2-3 saffron strands
1 tablespoon butter
1 large garlic clove, finely chopped
4 tablespoons chopped fresh mint
salt and freshly ground black pepper
yogurt and naan bread, to serve

onions   oil

yellow   ground   saffron
split peas   turmeric

yellow   garlic
split peas   ground beef

                                parsley

                chives

long-grain   yogurt
rice

mint   cilantro   butter

1 Chop one of the onions, then heat the oil in a large saucepan and sauté the onion until golden brown. Add the turmeric, split peas and 5 cups water, bring to a boil, then reduce the heat and simmer for about 20 minutes.

2 Grate the other onion into a bowl, add the ground beef and seasoning and mix well. Using your hands, form the mixture into small balls, about the size of walnuts. Carefully add to the pan and simmer for 10 minutes.

3 Add the rice, then stir in the parsley, cilantro, and chives and simmer, stirring frequently, for about 30 minutes, until the rice is tender. Infuse the saffron in 1 tablespoon boiling water.

4 Melt the butter in a small pan and gently sauté the garlic. Add the mint, stir briefly and sprinkle over the soup with the saffron and its liquid. Spoon the soup into warmed serving dishes and serve with yogurt and naan bread.

COOK'S TIP
Fresh spinach is also delicious in this soup. Add 2 ounces finely chopped spinach leaves to the soup with the parsley, cilantro and chives.

Stuffed Grape Leaves

Based on the Greek dolmades, but with a vegetarian brown rice stuffing, this makes an excellent appetizer, snack or buffet dish.

Makes about 40

INGREDIENTS

1 tablespoon sunflower oil
1 teaspoon sesame oil
1 onion, finely chopped
1¼ cups brown rice
2½ cups vegetable stock
1 small yellow bell pepper, seeded and finely chopped
½ cup dried apricots, finely chopped
2 lemons
⅔ cup pine nuts
3 tablespoons chopped fresh parsley
2 tablespoons chopped fresh mint
½ teaspoon apple pie spice
8-ounce package grape leaves preserved in brine, drained
2 tablespoons olive oil
freshly ground black pepper
lemon wedges, to garnish

TO SERVE

1¼ cups low-fat plain yogurt
2 tablespoons chopped mixed fresh herbs
cayenne pepper

1 Heat the sunflower and sesame oils together in a large saucepan. Add the onion and cook gently for 5 minutes to soften. Add the rice, stirring to coat the grains in oil. Pour in the stock, bring to a boil, then lower the heat, cover the pan and simmer for 30 minutes, or until the rice is tender but al dente.

yogurt

cayenne pepper

pine nuts

mint

mixed herbs

onion

sunflower oil

sesame oil

yellow bell pepper

parsley

olive oil

grape leaves

apple pie spice

brown rice

vegetable stock

dried apricots

lemons

2 Stir in the chopped pepper and apricots, with a little more stock if necessary. Replace the lid and cook for another 5 minutes. Grate the zest from one of the lemons, then squeeze both.

4 Bring a saucepan of water to a boil and blanch the grape leaves for 5 minutes. Drain the leaves well, then lay them shiny side down on a board. Cut out any coarse stalks. Place a heap of the rice mixture in the center of each grape leaf. Fold the stem end over, then the sides and pointed end, to make neat parcels.

3 Drain off any stock that has not been absorbed by the rice. Stir in the pine nuts, herbs, spice, grated lemon zest and half the juice. Season with pepper and set aside.

5 Pack the parcels closely together in a shallow serving dish. Mix the remaining lemon juice with the olive oil. Pour the mixture over the grape leaves, cover and chill before serving. Garnish with lemon wedges. Spoon the yogurt into a bowl, stir in the chopped herbs and sprinkle with a little cayenne. Serve with the stuffed grape leaves.

COOK'S TIP

If grape leaves are not available, the leaves of Swiss chard, young spinach or cabbage can be used instead.

Thai Rice Cakes with Spicy Dipping Sauce

Start cooking this dish the day before you want to serve it, as it involves some lengthy preparation.

Serves 4-6

INGREDIENTS
scant 1 cup jasmine rice
oil for deep-frying and greasing

FOR THE SPICY DIPPING SAUCE
6-8 dried chiles
½ teaspoon salt
2 shallots, chopped
2 garlic cloves, chopped
4 cilantro roots
10 white peppercorns
1 cup coconut milk
1 teaspoon shrimp paste
4 ounces ground pork
4 ounces cherry tomatoes, chopped
1 tablespoon fish sauce
1 tablespoon palm sugar
2 tablespoons tamarind juice
2 tablespoons coarsely chopped
    roasted peanuts
2 scallions, finely chopped
mint sprigs, to garnish

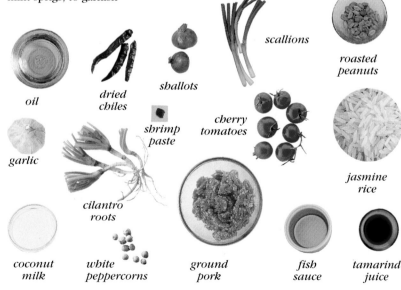

scallions

roasted peanuts

shallots

oil

dried chiles

shrimp paste

cherry tomatoes

garlic

coconut milk

cilantro roots

white peppercorns

ground pork

fish sauce

tamarind juice

jasmine rice

1 Make the sauce. Cut along the stem of each chile and remove most of the seeds. Soak the chiles in warm water for 20 minutes. Drain and transfer to a mortar. Add the salt and grind with a pestle until crushed. Add the shallots, garlic, cilantro roots and peppercorns. Pound to make a coarse paste.

2 Pour the coconut milk into a saucepan and boil until it begins to separate. Add the chile paste. Cook for 2–3 minutes, stir in the shrimp paste and cook for 1 minute. Add the pork and cook for 5–10 minutes, stirring well.

3 Add the tomatoes, fish sauce, palm sugar and tamarind juice. Simmer until the sauce thickens. Stir in the chopped peanuts and scallions. Remove from the heat and let cool. Chill the mixture overnight.

4 Wash the rice. Place in a saucepan, add 1¼ cups water and cover. Bring to a boil, reduce the heat and simmer for 12–15 minutes. Remove the lid and fluff up the rice. Turn out onto a lightly greased baking sheet and press down. Let dry overnight in a very low oven until dry and firm.

5 Remove the rice from the baking sheet and break into bite-size pieces. Heat the oil in a wok or deep fryer. Fry the rice cakes in batches for about 1 minute, until they puff up, taking care not to brown them too much. Remove and drain. Garnish with mint sprigs and serve with the spicy dipping sauce.

Sticky Rice Balls Filled with Chicken

These rice balls can be either steamed or deep-fried. The fried versions are crunchy and are excellent for serving at cocktail parties.

Makes about 30

INGREDIENTS
1 pound ground chicken
1 egg
1 tablespoon tapioca flour
4 scallions, finely chopped
2 tablespoons chopped cilantro
2 tablespoons fish sauce
pinch of sugar
1/3 cup glutinous (sticky) rice, cooked
banana leaves
oil for brushing
freshly ground black pepper
sweet chile sauce, to serve

FOR THE GARNISH
1 small carrot, shredded
1 red bell pepper, cut into strips
snipped chives

1 In a mixing bowl, combine the ground chicken, egg, tapioca flour, scallions and cilantro. Mix well and season with fish sauce, sugar and freshly ground black pepper.

scallions
glutinous rice
tapioca flour
oil
ground chicken
egg
sugar
cilantro
banana leaves
fish sauce
carrot
chives
sweet chile sauce
red bell pepper

COOK'S TIP
Try to find banana leaves for this recipe, as they impart their own subtle flavor of fine tea. The leaves are used in Thai cooking for wrapping foods as well as lining steamers.

2 Using chopsticks, spread the cooked sticky rice on a plate or baking sheet.

3 Place teaspoonfuls of some of the chicken mixture on the bed of rice, placing them evenly spaced apart. With damp hands, roll and shape this mixture in the rice to make balls about the size of a walnut. Repeat with the rest of the chicken mixture.

4 Line a bamboo steamer with banana leaves and lightly brush them with oil. Place the chicken balls on the leaves, spacing well apart to prevent them from sticking together. Steam over high heat for about 10 minutes, or until cooked. Remove and arrange on serving plates. Garnish with shredded carrot, red pepper and chives. Serve with sweet chile sauce as a dip.

Rice Balls Filled with Manchego Cheese

For a really impressive Spanish tapas-style snack, serve these delicious rice balls.

Serves 6

INGREDIENTS
1 globe artichoke
4 tablespoons butter
1 small onion, finely chopped
1 garlic clove, finely chopped
²⁄₃ cup risotto rice
scant 2 cups hot chicken stock
²⁄₃ cup freshly grated Parmesan cheese
5 ounces Manchego cheese, very finely diced
3-4 tablespoons coarse-grained cornmeal for polenta
olive oil for frying
salt and freshly ground black pepper
flat-leaf parsley, to garnish

artichoke *onion* *butter*
cornmeal *risotto rice*
chicken stock *garlic* *Parmesan cheese*
olive oil *Manchego cheese* *flat-leaf parsley*

1 Remove the stalk, leaves and choke to leave just the heart of the artichoke. Chop the heart finely.

2 Melt the butter in a saucepan and gently sauté the chopped artichoke heart, onion and garlic for 5 minutes, until softened. Stir in the rice and cook for about 1 minute.

COOK'S TIP
Manchego cheese is made with sheep's milk from La Mancha in Spain. It is ideal for grating or broiling.

3 Keeping the heat fairly high, gradually add the stock, stirring constantly until all the liquid has been absorbed and the rice is cooked—this should take about 20 minutes. Season well, then stir in the Parmesan. Transfer to a bowl. Let cool, then cover and chill for at least 2 hours.

4 Spoon about 1 tablespoon of the mixture into one hand, flatten slightly, and place a few pieces of diced Manchego cheese in the center. Shape to make a small ball. Flatten, then lightly roll in the cornmeal. Make about 12 cakes total. Fry in hot olive oil for 4–5 minutes, until the rice cakes are crisp and golden brown. Drain on paper towels and serve hot, garnished with parsley.

Rice Omelet

Rice is an unusual omelet filling in the West, but Japanese children love this recipe, and often top the omelets with ketchup.

Serves 4

INGREDIENTS
4 ounces skinless, boneless chicken
    thighs, cut into 1/2-inch cubes
7 teaspoons butter
1 small onion, chopped
1 carrot, chopped
2 shiitake mushrooms, stems
    removed, caps chopped
1 tablespoon finely chopped fresh
    parsley
3/4 cup Japanese rice, cooked
2 tablespoons ketchup
6 large eggs
4 tablespoons milk
salt and freshly ground black or white
    pepper
fresh parsley sprigs, to garnish
ketchup, to serve (optional)

chicken
thighs

onion

butter

mushrooms

carrot

milk

Japanese
rice

ketchup

parsley

eggs

1 Season the chicken with salt and pepper. Melt 1 1/2 teaspoons butter in a frying pan. Sauté the onion for 1 minute, then add the chicken and sauté until the chicken is white and cooked. Add the carrots and mushrooms, stir-fry over moderate heat until soft, then add the parsley. Set this mixture aside and wipe the frying pan clean.

2 Melt 1 1/2 teaspoons butter in the frying pan, add the rice and stir well. Mix in the sautéed ingredients, ketchup and pepper. Stir well, adding salt to taste if necessary. Keep the mixture warm. Beat the eggs lightly, then add the milk, 1/2 teaspoon salt and pepper.

COOK'S TIP

Shiitake mushrooms are the most popular ones in Japan. They have a good flavor, especially when dried. If using dried, soak them in a bowl of cold water for 20 minutes, placing a small saucer on top to keep the mushrooms submerged. Drain, but keep the soaking water if you like, as it makes a good stock.

3 Melt 1 teaspoon butter in an omelet pan over moderate heat. Pour in a quarter of the egg mixture and stir it briefly with a fork, then let set for 1 minute. Top with a quarter of the rice mixture.

4 Fold the omelet over the rice and slide it to the edge of the pan to shape it into a curve. Do not cook the omelet too much. Invert the omelet onto a warmed plate, cover with paper towels and press neatly into a rectangular shape. Cook another three omelets from the remaining ingredients. Serve immediately with ketchup drizzled on top, if you like. Garnish with parsley.

Rice Croquettes

These delicious croquettes are actually made from paella and are served as tapas, a snack or an appetizer, in Spain. The paella is cooked from scratch here, but you can use leftover paella instead.

Serves 4

INGREDIENTS
pinch of saffron strands
$\frac{2}{3}$ cup white wine
2 tablespoons olive oil
1 small onion, finely chopped
1 garlic clove, finely chopped
$\frac{2}{3}$ cup risotto rice
$1\frac{1}{4}$ cups hot chicken stock
2 ounces cooked shrimp, peeled, deveined and roughly chopped
2 ounces cooked chicken, roughly chopped
$\frac{1}{2}$ cup tiny peas, thawed if frozen
2 tablespoons freshly grated Parmesan cheese
1 egg, beaten
2 tablespoons milk
$1\frac{1}{2}$ cups fresh white bread crumbs
vegetable or olive oil, for frying
salt and freshly ground black pepper
fresh flat-leaf parsley, to garnish

risotto rice

chicken stock

saffron

white wine

olive oil

garlic

onion

egg

parsley

Parmesan cheese

oil

shrimp

cooked chicken

tiny peas

milk

bread crumbs

I Stir the saffron into the wine in a small bowl and set aside. Heat the oil in a heavy saucepan and gently sauté the onion and garlic for 5 minutes, until softened. Stir in the rice and cook for another minute.

2 Keeping the heat fairly high, add the wine and saffron mixture to the pan, stirring until it has all been absorbed. Gradually add the stock, stirring until all the liquid has been absorbed and the rice is cooked—this should take about 20 minutes.

3 Stir in the shrimp, chicken, peas and freshly grated Parmesan and stir well, cooking for 2–3 minutes. Season to taste with salt and pepper. Allow to cool slightly, then use two tablespoons to shape the mixture into 16 small croquettes.

4 Mix the egg and milk in a shallow bowl. Spread out the bread crumbs on a large, flat plate. Dip the croquettes in the egg mixture, then roll them in the bread crumbs to coat them. Heat the oil in a large frying pan. Fry the croquettes for 4–5 minutes, until crisp and golden brown. Drain on paper towels and serve hot, garnished with a sprig of flat-leaf parsley.

Sushi

This recipe shows one of the simplest forms of rolled sushi. You will need a bamboo mat (*makisu*) for the rolling process.

Makes 12 rolls or 72 slices

INGREDIENTS
6 sheets yaki-nori seaweed

FOR THE FILLING
7 ounces raw tuna
7 ounces raw salmon
$\frac{1}{2}$ cucumber, quartered lengthwise
    and seeds removed
wasabi paste (green horseradish)
gari (pickled ginger), to garnish
Japanese soy sauce, to serve

FOR THE SUSHI RICE
3 tablespoons rice vinegar
3 tablespoons sugar
2 teaspoons sea salt
$1\frac{3}{4}$ cups Japanese rice, cooked

yaki-nori seaweed

tuna

sea salt

salmon

cucumber

wasabi paste

rice vinegar

soy sauce

Japanese rice

sugar

1 To prepare the sushi rice, first make a dressing by heating the vinegar in a small saucepan, with a lid to keep in the strong vapors. Add the sugar and salt and dissolve. Let cool. Spread the cooked rice on a bamboo mat or tray. Pour on the dressing and fluff with chopsticks or a fork. Let cool.

2 Cut the nori in half lengthwise. Place a sheet of nori, shiny side down, on a bamboo mat on a cutting board. Divide the cooked rice in half, then mark each half into 6 pieces, making 12 portions in all. Spread one portion of rice over the nori with your fingers, leaving a $\frac{1}{2}$-inch space uncovered at the top and bottom of the nori.

3 Cut the tuna, the salmon and the cucumber into four long sticks each. The sticks should be the same length as the long side of the nori and the ends should measure $\frac{1}{2}$ inch square. Spread a little wasabi paste in a horizontal line along the middle of the rice and lay a stick of tuna on top.

COOK'S TIP

Japanese ingredients can be found in specialty food shops. When you buy the raw fish, make sure that it is for sashimi, or for use as raw fish, which means it must be particularly clean and fresh. You may be unaccustomed to using some of the ingredients included in this recipe. Take care when using wasabi paste, as it is extremely hot. It is also worth noting that Japanese soy sauce is different from the Chinese version, so do try to locate it for this recipe.

4 Holding the mat and the edge of the nori nearest to you, roll up the nori and rice tightly into a tube with the tuna in the middle. Use the mat as a guide— do not roll it into the food.

5 Carefully roll the sushi off the mat. Make 11 more rolls in the same way, four filled with tuna, four with salmon and four with cucumber. Do not use wasabi with the cucumber, as the paste will make it discolor and soften. Use a wet knife to cut each roll into six slices and set them on a platter. Wipe and rinse the knife occasionally between cuts. Garnish the sushi with gari, to refresh the palate between bites, and serve with soy sauce.

Paella

Based on the classic Spanish recipe, seafood and bacon are cooked with aromatic saffron rice.

Serves 6

INGREDIENTS
2 tablespoons olive oil
2 red bell peppers, seeded and
    roughly chopped
2 onions, roughly chopped
2 garlic cloves, crushed
4 ounces lean bacon, roughly
    chopped
1³/₄ cups long-grain rice
pinch of saffron strands
2 cups vegetable or chicken stock
1¹/₄ cups dry white wine
12 ounces ripe tomatoes
1 pound mixed cooked seafood, such
    as shrimp, mussels and squid
1 cup peas, thawed if frozen
3 tablespoons chopped fresh parsley
salt and freshly ground black pepper
whole cooked shrimp and mussels in
    their shells, to garnish

1 Heat half the olive oil in a paella pan or large flameproof casserole. Cook the chopped peppers for about 3 minutes, remove with a slotted spoon and drain on paper towels. Add the rest of the oil and cook the onions, garlic and bacon for about 5 minutes, or until the onions have softened slightly, stirring regularly.

garlic

tomatoes   onion   red bell peppers

mussels   white wine   parsley

stock

peas   cooked seafood

shrimp   bacon   saffron

 olive oil   long-grain rice

2 Add the rice and cook for 1 minute. Stir in the saffron, stock, wine and seasoning. Boil, then simmer, covered, for 12–15 minutes. Stir occasionally.

3 Meanwhile, plunge the tomatoes into a bowl of boiling water, then into cold water, and peel them. Quarter the tomatoes and scoop out the seeds. Roughly chop the flesh.

4 When the rice is cooked and most of the liquid has been absorbed, stir the tomatoes, seafood, peas and peppers into the mixture and heat gently, stirring occasionally, for 5 minutes, or until piping hot. Stir in the parsley and adjust the seasoning before serving, garnished with the whole cooked shrimp and mussels.

Kedgeree

This classic rice dish is often served for breakfast in England.

Serves 6

INGREDIENTS
1 pound mixed smoked fish
1¼ cups milk
1 cup long-grain rice
1 slice of lemon
4 tablespoons butter
1 teaspoon medium curry powder
½ teaspoon freshly grated nutmeg
1 tablespoon chopped fresh parsley
salt and freshly ground black pepper
flat-leaf parsley sprigs, to garnish

TO SERVE
2 hard-boiled eggs, quartered
slices of hot buttered toast

smoked fish

parsley

nutmeg

long-grain rice

lemon slice

butter

curry powder

milk

eggs

1 Poach the uncooked smoked fish in milk for 10 minutes, or until it flakes (see Cook's Tip). Drain off the milk and flake the fish. Mix with the other smoked fish.

2 Cook the rice in boiling water together with a slice of lemon for about 10 minutes, until just cooked. Drain well.

COOK'S TIP

You can use a variety of smoked fish. Cod and haddock are cold-smoked and must be poached. Mackerel and trout are hot-smoked and can be added next. If you are using smoked salmon, it can be added at this second stage even though it is cold-smoked.

3 Melt the butter in a large, heavy saucepan and add the rice and fish. Shake the saucepan to mix all the ingredients together thoroughly.

4 Stir in the curry powder, nutmeg, parsley and seasoning. Serve garnished with sprigs of parsley, quartered eggs and slices of hot buttered toast.

Jambalaya

This Cajun dish comes from the Deep South of the United States. It contains a wonderful combination of rice, meat and fish, with a kick of chile. If you like really spicy food, add a little more chile powder.

Serves 6

INGREDIENTS

1 pound skinless, boneless chicken
    thighs
8 ounces chorizo or spicy sausages
5 celery ribs
1 red bell pepper, seeded
1 green bell pepper, seeded
about 2 tablespoons oil
2 onions, roughly chopped
2 garlic cloves, crushed
2 teaspoons mild chile powder
$\frac{1}{2}$ teaspoon ground ginger
$1\frac{2}{3}$ cups long-grain rice
$3\frac{3}{4}$ cups chicken stock
6 ounces peeled cooked shrimp
salt and freshly ground black pepper
12 cooked shrimp in shells, with
    heads removed, to garnish

peeled shrimp   *chorizo*   *celery*

chicken thighs   *long-grain rice*   *ground ginger*

cooked shrimp   *oil*   *chicken stock*

garlic   *onions*   *green and red bell peppers*   *chile powder*

1   Cut the chicken and chorizo or spicy sausages into small, bite-size pieces. Cut the celery and peppers into thin 2-inch strips and set aside.

2   Heat the oil in a very large frying pan or large saucepan and cook the chicken until golden. Remove with a slotted spoon and drain on paper towels Cook the chorizo for 2 minutes and drain on paper towels.

3   Add the celery and peppers and cook for 3–4 minutes, until the vegetables begin to soften and turn golden. Drain on paper towels. Add a little more oil to the pan, if needed, and cook the onions and garlic for 3 minutes.

4   Stir in the chile powder and ginger and cook for 1 minute more.

5   Add the rice. Cook for 1 minute, until it begins to look translucent. Stir in the stock, replace the chicken and bring to a boil. Cover, then simmer for 12–15 minutes, stirring occasionally, until the rice is tender and the liquid has been absorbed. Add a little more water, if necessary, during cooking.

6   Gently stir the chorizo, peppers, celery and peeled shrimp into the rice. Cook over low heat, turning the mixture over with a large spoon, until piping hot. Adjust the seasoning and serve, garnished with the whole shrimp.

Middle Eastern Fish with Rice

This Arabic fish dish, *sayadieh*, is very popular in Lebanon.

Serves 4-6

INGREDIENTS
juice of 1 lemon
3 tablespoons oil
2 pounds cod steaks
4 large onions, chopped
1 teaspoon ground cumin
2 or 3 saffron strands
4 cups fish stock
2¼ cups long-grain rice
⅔ cup pine nuts, lightly toasted
salt and freshly ground black pepper
fresh parsley, to garnish

lemon *oil* *saffron*

cod *onions*

long-grain rice *ground cumin*

parsley *pine nuts*

fish stock

1 Mix together the lemon juice and 1 tablespoon of the oil in a shallow dish. Add the fish steaks, turning to coat thoroughly, then cover and let marinate for 30 minutes. Heat the remaining oil in a large saucepan or flameproof casserole and sauté the onions, stirring occasionally, for 5–6 minutes, until golden.

VARIATION

You can try this recipe using some other firm-fleshed fish, such as swordfish, if you like. You can also use any type of long-grain rice. Brown rice would make a particularly healthy option. If using, add some extra water with the stock and add more during cooking if necessary.

2 Drain the fish, reserving the marinade, and add to the pan. Sauté for 1–2 minutes on each side until lightly golden, then add the cumin, saffron strands and a little salt and pepper.

4 Transfer the fish to a plate and add the rice to the stock. Bring to a boil, then reduce the heat and simmer gently for 15 minutes, until nearly all the stock has been absorbed. Add extra water if necessary, a little at a time.

3 Pour in the fish stock and the reserved marinade and bring to a boil. Let simmer gently over low heat for about 5 minutes, until the fish is almost cooked.

5 Arrange the fish on the rice and cover. Steam over low heat for 10–15 minutes. Transfer the fish to a plate, then spoon the rice onto a large flat dish and arrange the fish on top. Sprinkle with toasted pine nuts and garnish with fresh parsley.

Indonesian Fried Rice

This fried rice dish makes an ideal supper on its own or even as an accompaniment. It is a very quick meal to prepare, as the rice is already cooked.

Serves 4

INGREDIENTS

4 shallots, roughly chopped
1 red chile, seeded and chopped
1 garlic clove, chopped
thin sliver of dried shrimp paste
3 tablespoons oil
8 ounces boneless lean pork, cut into fine strips
1 cup long-grain rice, boiled and cooled
3 or 4 scallions, thinly sliced
4 ounces cooked peeled shrimp
2 tablespoons sweet soy sauce
chopped cilantro and fine cucumber shreds, to garnish

chile

shallots

shrimp

scallions

pork

long-grain rice

oil

dried shrimp paste   *soy sauce*   *garlic*

1 In a mortar, pound the shallots, chile, garlic and shrimp paste with a pestle until they form a paste.

2 Heat a wok until hot, add 2 tablespoons of the oil and swirl it around. Add the pork and stir-fry for 2–3 minutes. Remove the pork from the wok, set aside and keep hot.

3 Add the remaining oil to the wok. When hot, add the spiced shallot paste and stir-fry for about 30 seconds.

4 Reduce the heat. Add the rice, scallions and shrimp. Stir-fry for 2–3 minutes. Add the pork and sprinkle with the soy sauce. Stir-fry until piping hot. Serve garnished with the chopped cilantro and cucumber shreds.

Chicken Paella

There are many variations on the basic paella recipe. Any seasonal vegetables can be added, as can mussels and other seafood.

Serves 4

INGREDIENTS
4 chicken legs (thighs and drumsticks)
4 tablespoons olive oil
1 large onion, finely chopped
1 garlic clove, crushed
1 teaspoon ground turmeric
4 ounces chorizo or smoked ham
1¼ cups long-grain rice
2½ cups chicken stock
4 tomatoes, peeled, seeded and chopped
1 red bell pepper, seeded and sliced
1 cup frozen peas
salt and freshly ground black pepper

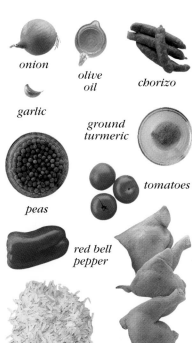

onion

olive oil

chorizo

garlic

ground turmeric

peas

tomatoes

red bell pepper

long-grain rice

chicken

chicken stock

1 Preheat the oven to 350°F. Cut the chicken legs in half.

2 Heat the oil in a 12-inch paella pan or large flameproof casserole and brown the chicken pieces on both sides. Add the onion and garlic and stir in the turmeric. Cook for 2 minutes.

3 Slice the chorizo or dice the ham and add to the pan together with the rice and stock. Bring to a boil and season to taste. Remove from the stove, cover and bake for about 15 minutes.

4 Remove from the oven and add the tomatoes, red pepper and frozen peas. Return to the oven and cook for another 10–15 minutes, or until the chicken is tender and the rice has absorbed the stock. Serve hot.

Poussins with Dirty Rice

The rice in this Cajun dish is called "dirty" because of the color the chicken livers give it. It may look dirty—but it tastes delicious.

Serves 4

INGREDIENTS

¼ cup oil
¼ cup all-purpose flour
6 tablespoons butter
1 large onion, chopped
2 celery ribs, chopped
1 green bell pepper, seeded and
   diced
2 garlic cloves, crushed
7 ounces ground pork
8 ounces chicken livers, trimmed
   and sliced
dash of Tabasco sauce
1¼ cups chicken stock
4 scallions, shredded
3 tablespoons chopped fresh parsley
1¼ cups long-grain rice, freshly
   cooked
2 bay leaves, halved
4 poussins (young, small chickens)
1 lemon
salt and freshly ground black pepper

1 Heat half the oil in a small, heavy saucepan and stir in the flour to make a roux. When it is a chestnut-brown color, remove the pan from the heat and place it immediately on a cold surface. Heat the remaining oil with 4 tablespoons of the butter in a frying pan and stir-fry the onion, celery and pepper for 5 minutes.

2 Add the garlic and pork and stir-fry for 5 minutes, breaking up the pork with a spoon so that it cooks evenly. Add the chicken livers and stir-fry for 3 minutes, until they have all changed color. Season and add a dash of Tabasco sauce.

3 Stir the roux into the stir-fried mixture, then gradually add the stock. When the mixture bubbles, cover and simmer for 30 minutes, stirring occasionally. Then uncover and cook for another 15 minutes, stirring frequently.

oil

flour

butter

garlic

Tabasco sauce

onion

chicken stock

celery

ground pork

chicken livers

bay leaves

green bell pepper

parsley

scallions

poussins

lemon

long-grain rice

4 Preheat the oven to 400°F. Mix the scallions and parsley into the meat mixture and stir it all into the cooked rice. Put ½ bay leaf and about 1 tablespoon of the rice mixture into each poussin. Rub the outsides with the remaining butter and season well.

5 Put the birds on a rack in a roasting pan, squeeze the juice from the lemon over them and roast for 35–40 minutes, basting twice with the pan juices. Put the remaining rice mixture in a shallow ovenproof dish, cover it and place on a low shelf in the oven for the last 15–20 minutes of the birds' cooking time. Serve the birds on a bed of dirty rice with the roasting pan juices (drained of fat) poured over them.

COOK'S TIP
You can substitute quail for the poussins, in which case offer two per person and stuff each little bird with 2 teaspoons of the dirty rice before roasting for about 20 minutes.

Thai Fried Rice

This hot and spicy dish is easy to prepare and makes a meal in itself. The delicate balance of flavors is exquisite.

Serves 4

INGREDIENTS

1¼ cups jasmine rice
3 tablespoons oil
1 onion, chopped
1 small red bell pepper, seeded and
   cut into ¾-inch cubes
12 ounces skinless, boneless chicken
   breasts, cut into ¾-inch cubes
1 garlic clove, crushed
1 tablespoon mild curry paste
½ teaspoon paprika
½ teaspoon ground turmeric
2 tablespoons Thai fish sauce
   (nam pla)
2 eggs, beaten
salt and freshly ground black pepper
fried fresh basil leaves, to garnish

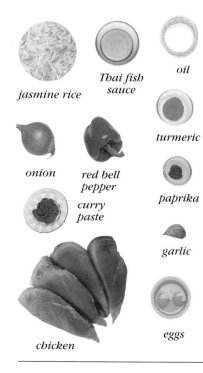

jasmine rice

Thai fish sauce

oil

onion

red bell pepper

curry paste

turmeric

paprika

garlic

chicken

eggs

1 Place the rice in a sieve and wash well under cold running water. Put the rice in a heavy pan with 6¼ cups boiling water. Return to a boil, then simmer, uncovered, for 8–10 minutes. Drain well. Spread out the grains on a baking sheet and let cool.

2 Heat a wok until hot. Add 2 tablespoons of the oil and swirl it around. Add the onion and pepper and stir-fry for 1 minute, until the onion just begins to soften slightly.

3 Add the chicken, garlic, curry paste, paprika and turmeric and stir-fry for 4–5 minutes, stirring well to evenly distribute the flavors and the paste.

4 Reduce the heat to medium and add the cooled rice, fish sauce and seasoning. Stir-fry for 2–3 minutes, until the rice is very hot.

5 Make a well in the center of the rice and add the remaining oil. When hot, add the beaten eggs, let cook for about 2 minutes, until lightly set, then stir into the rice.

6 Scatter the fried basil leaves over the top and serve at once.

VARIATION
Add ¼ cup frozen peas to the chicken in step 3, if you wish.

Chicken Biryani

In India, this dish is mainly prepared for important occasions, and is truly fit for royalty. Every cook has a subtle variation, which is kept a closely guarded secret.

Serves 4-6

INGREDIENTS

3 pounds skinless, boneless chicken breasts, cut into large pieces
4 tablespoons biryani masala paste
2 green chiles, chopped
1 tablespoon crushed fresh ginger
4 garlic cloves, crushed
2 ounces cilantro, chopped
6-8 fresh mint leaves, chopped, or 1 teaspoon mint sauce
²/₃ cup plain yogurt, beaten
2 tablespoons tomato paste
4 onions, finely sliced, deep-fried and crushed
salt, to taste
2¼ cups basmati rice, washed and drained
1 teaspoon black cumin seeds
1 piece cinnamon stick, 2 inches long
4 green cardamom pods
2 black cardamom pods
oil, for frying
4 large potatoes, peeled and quartered
1½ cups mixed milk and water
½ teaspoon saffron powder, mixed with 6 tablespoons milk
2 tablespoons ghee or unsalted butter

FOR THE GARNISH

ghee or unsalted butter, for shallow-frying
½ cup cashew nuts
⅓ cup golden raisins
2 hard-boiled eggs, quartered
deep-fried onion slices

1 Mix the chicken with the next 10 ingredients in a large bowl and allow to marinate for about 2 hours. Place in a large, heavy pan and cook gently for about 10 minutes. Set aside.

2 Bring a large saucepan of water to a boil. Add the rice, cumin seeds, cinnamon stick and cardamom, remove from the heat and let soak for 5 minutes. Drain well. Remove the cinnamon and cardamom at this stage, if you like.

3 Heat the oil for frying in a frying pan and fry the potatoes until they are evenly browned on all sides. Drain the potatoes on paper towels and set aside until needed.

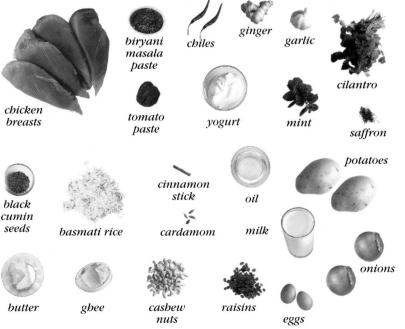

chicken breasts

biryani masala paste

chiles

ginger

garlic

cilantro

tomato paste

yogurt

mint

saffron

black cumin seeds

basmati rice

cinnamon stick

cardamom

oil

milk

potatoes

onions

butter

ghee

cashew nuts

raisins

eggs

4 Place half the rice on top of the chicken mixture in the pan in an even layer. Top with an even layer of potatoes. Put the remaining rice mixture on top of the potatoes and spread out to make an even layer. Sprinkle the milk and water mixture all over the top of the rice.

5 Make holes on the top with the handle of a spoon and pour a little saffron milk into each one. Add a few pats of ghee or butter, cover and cook over low heat for 35–45 minutes.

6 While the biryani is cooking, make the garnish. Heat a little ghee or butter in a frying pan and fry the cashew nuts and raisins until the raisins swell. Drain and set aside. When the biryani is ready, gently toss the rice, chicken and potatoes together. Garnish with the nut mixture, hard-boiled eggs and fried onion slices and serve hot.

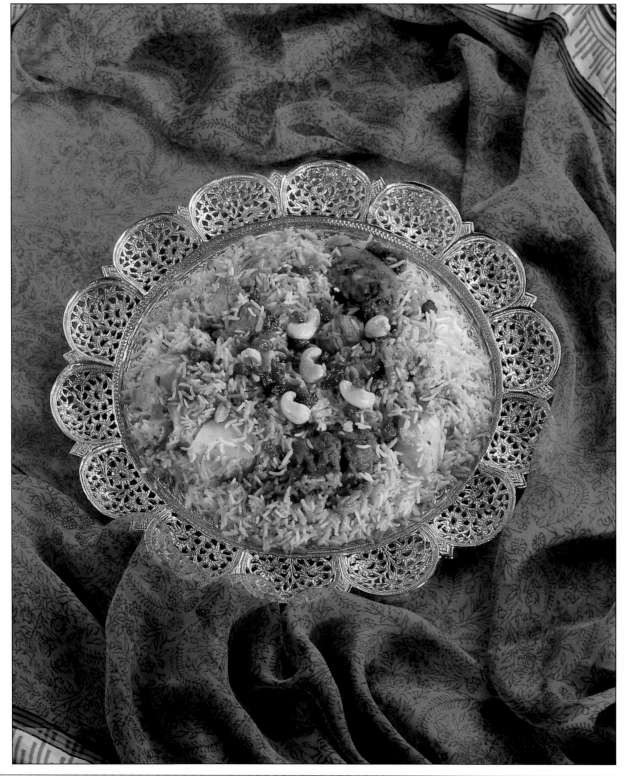

Nasi Goreng

This dish is originally from Thailand, but it can easily be adapted by adding any cooked ingredients that are at hand. Crispy shrimp crackers make an ideal accompaniment.

Serves 4

INGREDIENTS

1¼ cups long-grain rice
2 eggs
2 tablespoons oil
1 green chile
2 scallions, roughly chopped
2 garlic cloves, crushed
8 ounces cooked chicken
8 ounces cooked shrimp, peeled
3 tablespoons dark soy sauce
scallion shreds, to garnish
shrimp crackers, to serve

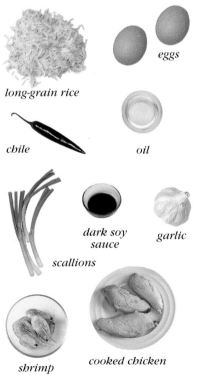

long-grain rice

eggs

chile

oil

dark soy sauce

garlic

scallions

shrimp

cooked chicken

1 Rinse and drain the rice and place in a saucepan together with 2½ cups water. Bring to a boil, cover with a tight-fitting lid and cook over low heat for 10–12 minutes. Rinse the rice with cold water through a sieve to cool it.

2 Lightly beat the eggs. Heat 1 tablespoon of oil in a small frying pan and swirl in the beaten egg. When cooked on one side, flip over and cook on the other side. Remove from the pan and let cool. Cut the omelet into thin strips and set aside.

3 Carefully remove the seeds from the chile and chop finely, wearing rubber gloves to protect your hands if necessary. Always keep hands away from eyes when chopping chiles. Place the scallions, chile and garlic in a food processor and blend to a paste.

4 Heat the wok, then add the remaining oil. When the oil is hot, add the chile paste and stir-fry for 1 minute.

5 Add the cooked chicken and shrimp and stir-fry until hot, making sure that the paste coats the chicken and shrimp evenly.

6 Add the cooked rice and stir-fry for 3–4 minutes, until piping hot. Stir in the omelet strips and soy sauce and garnish with scallion shreds. Serve with shrimp crackers.

Red Beans and Rice with Salt Pork

This classic Cajun dish is worth making in large quantities because of the long cooking time. It makes a splendid supper-party dish served with sausages and a green salad.

Serves 8–10

INGREDIENTS

2 cups dried red kidney beans,
    soaked in cold water overnight,
    rinsed and drained
2 bay leaves
2 tablespoons oil, bacon fat or lard
1 onion, chopped
2 garlic cloves, finely chopped
2 celery ribs, sliced
8-ounce piece of salt pork or raw ham
2¼ cups long-grain rice
3 tablespoons chopped fresh parsley
salt and freshly ground black pepper

red kidney
beans

bay
leaves

oil

onion

garlic

celery

parsley

long-grain
rice

ham

1 Place the beans in a large saucepan with cold water to cover. Boil rapidly for 10 minutes. Drain and rinse the beans and the pan. Return the beans to the pan, add the bay leaves and cover with cold water. Bring to a boil, reduce the heat and simmer for 30 minutes.

4 Place the rice in a pan and add 3 cups water. Stir in 1 teaspoon salt. Bring to a boil, stirring occasionally, then cover the pan with a tight-fitting lid and let cook over very low heat for about 15 minutes. Without lifting the lid, turn off the heat and set aside the rice for a further 5–10 minutes.

2 Meanwhile, heat the oil, fat or lard in a frying pan and cook the onion, garlic and celery gently, stirring frequently, until the onion is soft and translucent. Add the mixture to the beans.

3 Add the piece of salt pork or ham to the beans, pushing well down. Bring back to a boil and simmer, adding water as necessary, for 45 minutes, until the beans are very tender. Add salt, if necessary, 15–20 minutes before the end of the cooking time.

5 Lift out the piece of salt pork or ham and dice it, removing the fat and rind.

6 Drain the beans and adjust the seasoning. Stir the meat into the beans. Fluff up the rice and stir in the parsley. Serve with the beans on top.

Lamb Pilaf

In the Caribbean, rice is often cooked with meat and coconut milk, giving a deliciously rich and creamy texture. Sweet potato chips would make an ideal accompaniment, and are easily made by deep-frying thin slices of the vegetable until crisp.

Serves 4

INGREDIENTS

1 pound stewing lamb
1 tablespoon curry powder
1 onion, chopped
2 garlic cloves, crushed
$1/2$ teaspoon dried thyme
$1/2$ teaspoon dried oregano
1 fresh or dried chile, seeded and
    chopped
2 tablespoons butter or margarine,
    plus extra for serving
$2^{1}/2$ cups beef or chicken stock or
    coconut milk
1 teaspoon freshly ground black
    pepper
2 tomatoes, chopped
2 teaspoons sugar
2 tablespoons chopped scallions
$2^{1}/4$ cups basmati rice
scallion strips, to garnish

lamb

curry powder

onion

thyme

oregano

basmati rice

scallions

butter

stock

sugar

pepper

tomatoes

chile

garlic

1 Cut the meat into cubes, discarding any excess fat and gristle. Place in a shallow glass or ceramic dish.

2 Sprinkle with the curry powder, onion, garlic, herbs and chile. Stir well. Cover loosely with plastic wrap and set aside to marinate in a cool place for 1 hour. Melt the butter or margarine in a saucepan and sauté the lamb on all sides for 5–10 minutes. Add the stock or coconut milk. Bring to a boil, lower the heat and simmer for 35 minutes, or until the meat is tender.

3 Add the black pepper, tomatoes, sugar, scallions and rice, stir well and reduce the heat. Make sure that the rice is covered by 1 inch of liquid; add a little water if necessary. Simmer the pilaf for 25 minutes, or until the rice is cooked, then stir a little extra butter or margarine into the rice before serving. Garnish with scallion strips.

Wild Rice and Turkey Salad

A delicious and healthy salad that makes a perfect light lunch or supper dish. For a softer texture but a similar flavor, use a mixture of wild rice and long-grain rice and reduce the cooking time a little.

Serves 4

INGREDIENTS
³/₄ cup wild rice
2 celery ribs, thinly sliced
2 scallions, chopped
1 cup small button mushrooms, quartered
1 pounds cold cooked turkey breast, diced
¹/₂ cup vinaigrette dressing, made with walnut oil
4 fresh thyme sprigs
salt

TO SERVE
2 pears, peeled, halved and cored
3 tablespoons walnut pieces, toasted

1 Pour 4 cups cold water into a saucepan and add a pinch of salt. Bring to a boil. Add the wild rice to the pan and bring back to a boil. Cook for 45–50 minutes, until tender but firm and the grains have begun to split open. Drain well and set aside to cool.

wild rice

celery

turkey breast

scallions

pears

thyme

mushrooms

walnut pieces

VARIATION
You can use chicken instead of turkey breast with any vinaigrette dressing. Toast a selection of nuts for a different flavor, if you like.

2 Combine the wild rice with the celery, scallions, mushrooms and cooked turkey in a bowl.

3 Add the dressing and thyme and toss well together. Thinly slice the pear halves lengthwise without cutting through the stem end and spread the slices like a fan. Divide the salad among four plates. Garnish each with a fanned pear half and toasted walnuts.

Asian Fried Rice

This is a great way to use leftover cooked rice.
Make sure the rice is very cold before attempting
to fry it, as warm rice will become soggy. Some
supermarkets sell frozen cooked rice.

Serves 4-6

INGREDIENTS

5 tablespoons oil
4 ounces shallots, halved and
    thinly sliced
3 garlic cloves, crushed
1 red chile, seeded and finely
    chopped
6 scallions, finely chopped
1 red bell pepper, seeded and finely
    chopped
8 ounces white cabbage, finely
    shredded
6 ounces cucumber, finely chopped
½ cup peas, thawed if frozen
3 eggs, beaten
1 teaspoon tomato paste
2 tablespoons lime juice
¼ teaspoon Tabasco sauce
1¼ cups long-grain rice, cooked
    and cooled
1 cup cashew nuts, roughly chopped
about 2 tablespoons chopped
    cilantro, plus extra to garnish
salt and freshly ground black pepper

1 Heat half the oil in a large nonstick frying pan or wok and cook the shallots until very crisp and golden. Remove with a slotted spoon and drain well on paper towels.

2 Add the rest of the oil to the pan. Cook the garlic and chile for 1 minute. Add the scallions and pepper and cook for another 3–4 minutes.

3 Add the cabbage, cucumber and peas and cook for 2 minutes more.

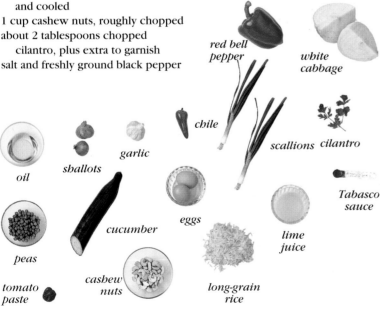

red bell
pepper

white
cabbage

chile

scallions   cilantro

garlic

oil

shallots

Tabasco
sauce

cucumber

eggs

lime
juice

peas

tomato
paste

cashew
nuts

long-grain
rice

4 Make a gap in the pan and add the beaten eggs. Scramble the eggs, stirring occasionally, and then stir them into the vegetables.

5 Add the tomato paste, lime juice and Tabasco and stir to combine.

6 Increase the heat and add the rice, cashew nuts and cilantro with plenty of seasoning. Stir-fry for 3–4 minutes, until piping hot. Serve garnished with the crisp shallots and extra cilantro.

Lentils and Rice

Lentils are cooked with whole and ground spices, potatoes, rice and onions here to produce an authentic Indian-style dish that makes a satisfying light but wholesome meal.

Serves 4

INGREDIENTS

²/₃ cup red split lentils
²/₃ cup basmati rice
1 large potato
1 large onion
2 tablespoons oil
4 whole cloves
¹/₄ teaspoon cumin seeds
¹/₄ teaspoon ground turmeric
2 teaspoons salt

basmati rice

oil

cumin seeds

ground turmeric

red split lentils

potato

salt

cloves   onion

1 Wash the lentils and rice in several changes of cold water. Place in a bowl and cover with water. Let soak for 15 minutes, then drain.

2 While the rice and lentils are soaking, peel the potato and rinse well. Cut it into 1-inch chunks. Peel the onion and cut it into thin slices.

3 Heat the oil in a large, heavy saucepan and fry the cloves and cumin seeds for 2 minutes, until the seeds are beginning to splutter.

4 Add the onion and potatoes and cook for 5 minutes, until slightly browned. Add the lentils and rice, with the turmeric and salt, and cook for 3 minutes.

5 Pour 2 cups water into the saucepan. Bring to a boil, cover tightly and simmer for 15–20 minutes, until all the water has been absorbed and the potatoes are tender. Let stand, covered, for about 10 minutes, then serve.

Vegetable Kedgeree

Crunchy green beans and mushrooms are the star ingredients in this vegetarian version of a rice dish traditionally made with fish as well as egg.

Serves 2

INGREDIENTS
²/₃ cup basmati rice
3 eggs
6 ounces greens beans, trimmed
4 tablespoons butter
1 onion, finely chopped
2 cups cremini mushrooms,
    quartered
2 tablespoons light cream
1 tablespoon chopped fresh parsley
salt and freshly ground black pepper

basmati rice

eggs

light cream

green beans

butter

onion

parsley

cremini mushrooms

1 Wash the rice several times under cold running water. Drain thoroughly. Bring a pan of water to a boil, add the rice and cook for 10–12 minutes, until tender. Drain thoroughly.

2 Half-fill a second pan with water, add the eggs and bring to a boil. Lower the heat and simmer for 8 minutes. Drain the eggs, cool them under cold running water, then remove the shells and rinse.

3 Bring another pan of water to a boil and cook the green beans for about 5 minutes. Drain, refresh under cold running water, then drain again.

4 Melt the butter in a large frying pan. Add the onion and mushrooms. Cook for 2–3 minutes over moderate heat.

5 Add the green beans and rice to the onion mixture. Stir lightly to mix. Cook for 2 minutes. Cut the hard-boiled eggs into wedges and carefully add them to the pan.

6 Stir in the cream and parsley, taking care not to break up the eggs. Reheat the kedgeree, but do not allow it to boil. Season with salt and pepper and serve at once.

Vegetable Pilaf

A delicious vegetable rice dish that also goes well with most Indian meat dishes.

Serves 4-6

INGREDIENTS
1¼ cups basmati rice
2 tablespoons oil
½ teaspoon cumin seeds
2 bay leaves
4 green cardamom pods
4 cloves
1 onion, finely chopped
1 carrot, finely chopped
½ cup peas, thawed if frozen
⅓ cup corn kernels, thawed if frozen
¼ cup cashew nuts, lightly fried
¼ teaspoon ground coriander
¼ teaspoon ground cumin
salt

ground coriander

peas

carrot

corn

cumin seeds

oil

bay leaves

onion

ground cumin

cardamom pods

cloves

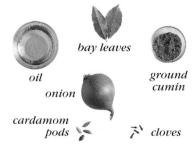
cashew nuts

basmati rice

1 Wash the basmati rice in several changes of cold water. Put in a bowl and cover with cold water. Let soak for 30 minutes.

2 Heat the oil in a large frying pan and fry the cumin seeds for 2 minutes. Add the bay leaves, cardamom and cloves and fry for 2 minutes.

3 Add the onion and cook for 5 minutes, until lightly browned.

4 Stir in the carrot and cook for 3–4 minutes.

5 Drain the rice and add to the pan with the peas, corn and cashew nuts. Cook for 4–5 minutes.

6 Pour in 2 cups cold water, then add the remaining spices and salt to taste. Bring to a boil, cover, then simmer over low heat for about 15 minutes, until all the water is absorbed. Let stand, covered, for 10 minutes before serving.

VARIATION

You can add your favorite vegetables, such as potatoes, to this recipe, if you like, although this particular vegetable will require a longer cooking time.

Stuffed Vegetables

Vegetables such as peppers make wonderful containers for savory fillings. Instead of sticking to one type of vegetable, serve a selection. Thick, creamy plain yogurt is the ideal accompaniment.

Serves 3-6

INGREDIENTS
1 eggplant
1 large green bell pepper
2 large tomatoes
1 large onion, chopped
2 garlic cloves, crushed
3 tablespoons olive oil
1 cup brown rice
2½ cups vegetable stock
1 cup pine nuts
⅓ cup currants
3 tablespoons chopped fresh dill
3 tablespoons chopped fresh parsley
1 tablespoon chopped fresh mint
extra olive oil, to sprinkle
salt and freshly ground black pepper
strained plain yogurt and fresh dill
    sprigs, to serve

eggplant

olive oil

garlic

green bell
pepper

brown rice

dill

parsley

tomatoes

onion

pine nuts

mint

yogurt

vegetable
stock

currants

1 Halve the eggplant, scoop out the flesh with a sharp knife and chop finely. Salt the insides of the shells and let drain upside down for 20 minutes while you prepare the other ingredients. Halve the pepper, seed and core.

2 Cut the tops from the tomatoes, scoop out the insides and chop roughly along with the tomato tops. Set the tomato shells aside. Cook the onion, garlic and chopped eggplant in the oil for 10 minutes, then stir in the rice and cook for 2 minutes. Add the tomato flesh, stock, pine nuts, currants and seasoning. Bring to a boil, cover and lower the heat. Simmer for 15 minutes, then stir in the herbs.

3 Preheat the oven to 375°F. Blanch the eggplant and pepper halves in boiling water for about 3 minutes, then drain them upside down on paper towels.

4 Spoon the rice filling into all six vegetable containers and place on a lightly greased shallow baking dish. Drizzle some olive oil over the stuffed vegetables and bake for 25–30 minutes. Serve hot, topped with spoonfuls of yogurt and the dill sprigs.

Pilaf with Omelet Rolls and Nuts

A wonderful mixture of textures—soft, fluffy rice with crunchy nuts and omelet rolls.

Serves 2

INGREDIENTS
scant 1 cup basmati rice
1 tablespoon sunflower oil
1 small onion, chopped
1 red bell pepper, finely diced
1½ cups hot vegetable stock
2 eggs
¼ cup salted peanuts
1 tablespoon soy sauce
salt and freshly ground black pepper
fresh parsley sprigs, to garnish

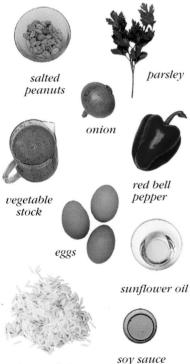

salted peanuts

parsley

onion

vegetable stock

red bell pepper

eggs

basmati rice

sunflower oil

soy sauce

1 Wash the rice several times under cold running water. Drain thoroughly. Heat half the oil in a large frying pan. Cook the onion and pepper for 2–3 minutes, then stir in the rice and stock, bring to a boil and cook for 10–12 minutes, until the rice is tender.

2 Meanwhile, beat the eggs lightly with salt and pepper to taste. Heat the remaining oil in a second large frying pan. Pour in the eggs and tilt the pan to cover the bottom thinly. Cook the omelet for 1 minute, then flip it over and cook the other side for 1 minute.

3 Slide the omelet onto a clean board and roll it up tightly. Cut the omelet roll into 8 slices.

4 Stir the peanuts and the soy sauce into the pilaf and add black pepper to taste. Turn the pilaf out into a serving dish, arrange the omelet rolls on top and garnish with the parsley. Serve at once.

Fruity Rice Salad

An appetizing and colorful rice salad combining many different flavors, ideal for a brown-bag lunch.

Serves 4-6

INGREDIENTS
1 cup mixed brown and wild rice
1 yellow bell pepper, seeded and diced
1 bunch scallions, chopped
3 celery ribs, chopped
1 large beefsteak tomato, chopped
2 green-skinned apples, chopped
$^3/_4$ cup dried apricots, chopped
$^2/_3$ cup raisins

FOR THE DRESSING
2 tablespoons unsweetened apple juice
2 tablespoons dry sherry
2 tablespoons light soy sauce
dash of Tabasco sauce
2 tablespoons chopped fresh parsley
1 tablespoon chopped fresh rosemary
salt and freshly ground black pepper

celery

mixed brown and wild rice

scallions

beefsteak tomato

apricots

apple juice

soy sauce

raisins *rosemary* *parsley*

sherry *Tabasco sauce* *apples* *yellow bell pepper*

1 Cook the rice in a large saucepan of lightly salted, boiling water for about 35 minutes, until tender. Rinse the rice under cold running water to cool quickly and drain thoroughly.

2 Place the pepper, scallions, celery, tomato, apples, apricots, raisins and the cooked rice in a large serving bowl and mix well.

3 To make the dressing, mix together the apple juice, sherry, soy sauce, Tabasco sauce, fresh herbs and seasoning in a small bowl.

4 Pour the dressing over the rice mixture and toss the ingredients together to mix. Serve immediately or cover and chill in the refrigerator until ready to serve.

Risotto with Asparagus

A fresh and delicious risotto is one of the great classic rice dishes. This recipe makes an elegant meal when asparagus is in season.

Serves 4-5

INGREDIENTS
8 ounces asparagus
3 cups vegetable or meat stock,
    preferably homemade
5 tablespoons butter
1 small onion, finely chopped
2 cups risotto rice
1 cup freshly grated Parmesan cheese
salt and freshly ground black pepper

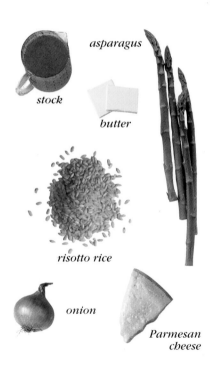

stock

asparagus

butter

risotto rice

onion

Parmesan cheese

COOK'S TIP
Parmesan cheese is ideal for cooking because it does not become stringy or rubbery when heated. It can be grated over many hot dishes, such as pasta and risotto, as well as added to cold salads. There are two basic types of Parmesan cheese—Parmigiano-Reggiano and Grana Padano—but the former is superior in quality.

1 Peel the lower stalks of the asparagus. Bring 3 cups of water to a boil in a large saucepan and blanch the asparagus for 5 minutes. Remove, reserving the cooking water, and rinse under cold water. Drain and cut each spear diagonally into 1½-inch pieces, separating the tip and next-highest sections from the stalks. Place the stock in a saucepan with 2½ cups of the asparagus cooking water. Heat the liquid to simmering, and keep it hot until it is needed.

2 Heat two-thirds of the butter in a large, heavy frying pan or casserole. Add the onion and cook until it is soft and golden. Stir in the asparagus stalks. Cook for 2–3 minutes. Add the rice, mixing well to coat the grains with butter. Cook for 1–2 minutes.

3 Stir in half a ladleful of the hot liquid. Stir constantly until the liquid has been absorbed. Add another half ladleful of the liquid and stir until it has also been absorbed. Continue stirring and adding the liquid, a little at a time, for about 10 minutes.

4 Add the remaining asparagus sections and continue cooking, stirring and adding the liquid until the rice is al dente. Total cooking time will be about 30 minutes. If you run out of stock, use hot water, but do not worry if the rice is ready before all the stock has been added. Remove the pan from the heat and stir in the remaining butter and the Parmesan. Add a little black pepper and salt to taste. Serve at once.

Risotto-Stuffed Eggplant with Spicy Tomato Sauce

Eggplant is a challenge to the creative cook and allows for some unusual recipe ideas. Here, they are stuffed and baked with a cheese and pine nut topping.

COOK'S TIP
If the eggplant shells do not stand level, cut a thin slice from the bottom. When browning the filled shells, use crumpled foil to support them.

Serves 4

INGREDIENTS
4 small eggplant
7 tablespoons olive oil
1 small onion, chopped
scant 1 cup risotto rice
3 cups hot vegetable stock
1 tablespoon white wine vinegar
1/3 cup freshly grated Parmesan cheese
2 tablespoons pine nuts
8 fresh basil sprigs, to garnish

FOR THE TOMATO SAUCE
1 1/4 cups thick passata or tomato paste
1 teaspoon mild curry paste
pinch of salt

eggplant

wine vinegar

onion *vegetable stock*

risotto rice

olive oil *Parmesan cheese*

curry paste *passata* *pine nuts*

1 Preheat the oven to 400°F. Cut the eggplant in half lengthwise and remove their flesh with a small knife. Brush the shells with 2 tablespoons of the oil, place on a baking sheet and bake for 6–8 minutes.

2 Chop the reserved eggplant flesh. Heat the remainder of the olive oil in a medium saucepan. Add the eggplant flesh and the onion and cook over gentle heat for 3–4 minutes, until just soft.

3 Add the rice, stir in the stock and let simmer, uncovered, for another 15 minutes. Stir in the vinegar.

4 Increase the oven temperature to 450°F. Spoon the rice into the eggplant shells, top with the cheese and pine nuts, return to the oven and brown for 5 minutes.

5 To make the sauce, mix the passata or tomato paste with the curry paste in a small pan. Heat through and add salt to taste.

6 Spoon the sauce onto four large serving plates and position two stuffed eggplant halves on each. Garnish with basil sprigs.

Leek, Mushroom and Lemon Risotto

A delicious risotto, packed full of flavor, makes a marvelous treat for friends and family.

Serves 4

INGREDIENTS

8 ounces trimmed leeks
2-3 cups cremini mushrooms
2 tablespoons olive oil
3 garlic cloves, crushed
6 tablespoons butter
1 large onion, roughly chopped
1³/₄ cups risotto rice
5 cups simmering vegetable stock
grated zest of 1 lemon
3 tablespoons lemon juice
²/₃ cup freshly grated Parmesan
    cheese
¹/₄ cup mixed chopped fresh chives
    and flat-leaf parsley
salt and freshly ground black pepper
lemon wedges, to serve

leeks

olive oil

mushrooms

lemon   butter

risotto rice

Parmesan cheese

onion

garlic   vegetable stock

parsley   chives

1 Wash the leeks well. Slice them in half lengthwise and chop them roughly. Wipe the mushrooms with paper towels and chop them roughly.

2 Heat the oil in a large saucepan and cook the garlic for 1 minute. Add the leeks, mushrooms and plenty of seasoning and cook over medium heat for about 10 minutes, or until softened and browned. Remove from the pan and set aside.

3 Add 2 tablespoons of the butter to the pan. As soon as it has melted, add the onion and cook over medium heat for 5 minutes, until softened and golden.

4 Stir in the rice and cook for about 1 minute, until the grains begin to look translucent and are coated in the fat. Add a ladleful of stock to the pan and cook gently, stirring occasionally, until the liquid has been absorbed.

5 Continue to add stock, a ladleful at a time, until all the stock has been absorbed. This should take 25–30 minutes. The risotto will turn thick and creamy and the rice should be tender but not sticky.

6 Just before serving, stir in the leeks, mushrooms, remaining butter, grated lemon zest and juice. Add half the grated Parmesan and herbs. Adjust the seasoning and sprinkle with the remaining Parmesan and herbs. Garnish with parsley, if you like, and serve with lemon wedges.

Shellfish Risotto with Mixed Mushrooms

The combination of shellfish and mushrooms in this creamy risotto is exquisite. Serve with chunks of hot ciabatta, if you like.

Serves 4

INGREDIENTS
8 ounces live mussels
8 ounces littleneck or carpet
    shell clams
3 tablespoons olive oil
1 onion, chopped
2-3 cups assorted wild and cultivated
    mushrooms, trimmed and sliced
2¼ cups risotto rice
5 cups hot chicken or vegetable stock
⅔ cup white wine
4 ounces cooked shrimp, deveined
    and heads and tails removed
1 squid, cleaned, trimmed and sliced
3 drops truffle oil (optional)
5 tablespoons chopped fresh parsley
    and chervil
celery salt and cayenne pepper

mushrooms

olive oil

white wine

risotto rice

stock

onion

parsley

shrimp

mussels

clams

truffle oil

squid

1 Scrub the mussels and clams and tap them with a knife. If any shells do not close, discard them. Set aside. Heat the oil in a large saucepan and cook the onion for 6–8 minutes, until soft but not browned.

COOK'S TIP
Use a mixture of mushrooms, such as cépes, chanterelles, hen-of-the-woods, horn of plenty, oyster and truffles. Wash all mushrooms carefully, particularly wild ones. It is worth noting that hen-of-the-woods mushrooms may need to be blanched in boiling salted water for 2-3 minutes before cooking, to remove their slight bitter taste. Also, use truffles sparingly, as they have a strong flavor.

2 Add the mushrooms and allow them to soften until their juices begin to run. Stir in the rice and heat through.

3 Pour in the stock and wine. Add the mussels, clams, shrimp and squid, stir gently and simmer for 15 minutes. If any of the mussels or clams do not open after cooking, discard them.

4 Remove from the heat. Add the truffle oil if using, and stir in the herbs. Cover tightly and let stand for 5–10 minutes, to allow all the flavors to blend. Season to taste with celery salt and a pinch of cayenne pepper and serve immediately.

Salmon Risotto with Cucumber and Tarragon

Arborio or Carnaroli rices are ideal for this simple and delicious risotto. Fresh tarragon and cucumber combine well to bring out the flavor of the salmon, making a particularly delicate and fragrant dish.

Serves 4

INGREDIENTS
2 tablespoons butter
1 small bunch of scallions, white
    parts only, chopped
$\frac{1}{2}$ cucumber, peeled, seeded and
    chopped
2 cups risotto rice
$3\frac{3}{4}$ cups chicken or fish stock
$\frac{2}{3}$ cup dry white wine
1-pound salmon fillet, skinned and
    diced
3 tablespoons chopped fresh tarragon

I Heat the butter in a large saucepan and add the scallions and cucumber. Cook for 2–3 minutes without coloring.

butter

scallions

salmon fillet

white wine

stock

cucumber

risotto rice

tarragon

VARIATION
Smoked salmon can be used instead of fresh. Buy end pieces, which are cheaper than slices, and cut them into bite-size pieces. Add right at the end, just before the standing time.

2 Add the rice, stock and wine, return to a boil and simmer uncovered for 10 minutes, stirring occasionally.

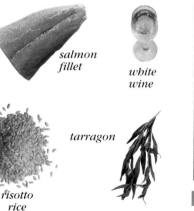

3 Stir in the diced salmon and tarragon. Continue cooking for another 5 minutes, then turn off the heat. Cover and let stand for 5 minutes before serving.

Risotto with Chicken

A classic combination of chicken and rice, cooked with prosciutto, white wine and Parmesan.

Serves 4

INGREDIENTS

2 tablespoons olive oil
8 ounces skinless, boneless chicken
  breast, cut into 1-inch cubes
1 onion, finely chopped
1 garlic clove, finely chopped
$\frac{1}{4}$ teaspoon saffron strands
2 ounces prosciutto, cut into thin
  strips
$2\frac{1}{4}$ cups risotto rice
$\frac{1}{2}$ cup dry white wine
$7\frac{1}{2}$ cups simmering chicken stock
2 tablespoons butter (optional)
$\frac{1}{3}$ cup freshly grated Parmesan
  cheese, plus more to serve
salt and freshly ground black pepper
flat-leaf parsley, to garnish

olive oil *onion* *garlic* *saffron*

chicken *risotto rice*

prosciutto

stock *white wine* *parsley*

butter *Parmesan cheese*

1 Heat the oil in a wide, heavy pan over moderately high heat. Add the chicken cubes and cook, stirring, until they start to turn white.

2 Reduce the heat to low and add the onion, garlic, saffron and prosciutto. Cook, stirring, until the onion is soft. Stir in the rice. Sauté for 1–2 minutes, stirring constantly.

3 Add the wine and bring to a boil. Simmer gently until almost all the wine has been absorbed. Add the simmering stock, a ladleful at a time, until absorbed; cook until the rice is just tender and the risotto is creamy.

4 Add the butter, if using, and the Parmesan cheese and stir in well. Season with salt and pepper to taste. Serve the risotto hot, sprinkled with a little more Parmesan, and garnish with parsley.

Risotto with Bacon and Tomato

A classic risotto, with plenty of onions, bacon and sun-dried tomatoes. You'll want to keep going back for more!

Serves 4

INGREDIENTS
8 sun-dried tomatoes in olive oil
10 ounces good-quality bacon
6 tablespoons butter
1 pound onions, roughly chopped
2 garlic cloves, crushed
1³/₄ cups risotto rice
1¹/₄ cups dry white wine
3³/₄ cups simmering vegetable stock
²/₃ cup freshly grated Parmesan
　　cheese
3 tablespoons mixed chopped fresh
　　chives and flat-leaf parsley
salt and freshly ground black pepper
flat-leaf parsley sprigs, to garnish
lemon wedges, to serve

flat-leaf parsley

bacon

chives

vegetable stock

butter

garlic

Parmesan cheese

sun-dried tomatoes

white wine

risotto rice

onions

lemon

1 Drain the sun-dried tomatoes and reserve 1 tablespoon of the oil. Roughly chop the tomatoes and set aside. Cut the bacon into 1-inch strips.

2 Heat the reserved sun-dried tomato oil in a large saucepan. Fry the bacon until well cooked and golden. Remove with a slotted spoon and drain on paper towels.

3 Add 2 tablespoons of the butter to the pan. When it melts, add the onions and garlic. Cook over medium heat for 10 minutes, until softened and golden brown.

4 Stir in the rice. Cook for 1 minute, until it turns translucent. Stir the wine into the simmering stock. Add a ladleful to the rice and cook gently until absorbed.

5 Stir in another ladleful of the stock and wine mixture and allow it to be absorbed again. Repeat this process until all the liquid is used up. This should take 25–30 minutes. The risotto will turn thick and creamy, and the rice should be tender but not sticky.

6 Just before serving, stir in the bacon, sun-dried tomatoes, half the Parmesan and herb, and the remaining butter. Adjust the seasoning (remember that the bacon may be quite salty) and serve sprinkled with the remaining Parmesan and herbs. Garnish with parsley and serve with lemon wedges.

SIDE DISHES

Egg Fried Rice

This is one of the most famous of rice side dishes. Use rice with a fairly firm texture. Ideally, the rice should be soaked in water for a short time before cooking.

Serves 4

INGREDIENTS
3 eggs
1 teaspoon salt
2 scallions, finely chopped
2-3 tablespoons oil
scant 1 cup long-grain rice, cooked
    and cooled
1 cup peas, thawed if frozen

scallions

peas

long-grain rice

oil

eggs

salt

1 In a bowl, lightly beat the eggs with a pinch of the salt and a few pieces of the chopped scallion. Heat a wok and when it is hot add some oil. When the oil is hot add the eggs and lightly scramble them.

2 Add the cooked rice and stir to make sure that each grain stays separate. Add the remaining salt, scallions and the peas. Mix well and stir-fry for a few minutes, until the rice is piping hot. Serve immediately.

Coconut Rice

This side dish is popular in Thailand, where jasmine rice is commonly eaten and coconut is used in many recipes. Rich and delicious, this tastes great with a tangy papaya salad.

Serves 4-6

INGREDIENTS
2¼ cups jasmine rice
2 cups coconut milk
½ teaspoon salt
2 tablespoons sugar
shredded fresh coconut, to garnish
    (optional)

fresh coconut

salt

jasmine rice

sugar

coconut milk

1 Wash the rice in several changes of cold water until it runs clear. Place the coconut milk, salt and sugar in a heavy saucepan. Add 1 cup water and stir in the rice. Cover and bring to a boil. Reduce the heat and simmer for 15–20 minutes, or until the rice is al dente.

2 Turn off the heat, cover and let the rice rest in the saucepan for 5–10 minutes. Fluff up the rice with chopsticks before serving. Garnish with shredded coconut, if you like.

Special Fried Rice

Special Fried Rice is a very popular rice recipe in China. Because it contains shrimp and ham, it can almost make a meal in itself.

Serves 4

INGREDIENTS

2 ounces cooked shrimp, peeled
2 ounces cooked ham
3 eggs
1 teaspoon salt
2 scallions, finely chopped, plus extra
    to garnish
4 tablespoons oil
1 cup peas, thawed if frozen
1 tablespoon light soy sauce
1 tablespoon Chinese rice wine or
    dry sherry
scant 1 cup long-grain rice, cooked

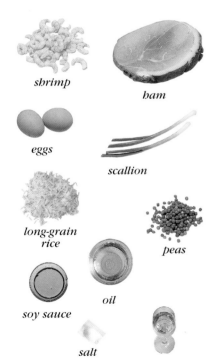

shrimp

ham

eggs

scallion

long-grain
rice

peas

oil

soy sauce

salt

sherry

1 Pat the cooked shrimp dry with paper towels, making sure no moisture remains. Cut the ham into small dice about the same size as the peas.

2 In a bowl, lightly beat the eggs with a pinch of the salt and a few pieces of the chopped scallions, using chopsticks or a fork.

COOK'S TIP

Chinese rice wine can be found in large supermarkets and Asian food shops.

3 Heat the wok, add about half of the oil and when it is hot, stir-fry the peas, shrimp and ham for about 1 minute. Add the soy sauce and rice wine or sherry. Transfer the mixture to a dish and keep hot.

4 Heat the remaining oil in the wok and scramble the eggs lightly. Add the rice and stir to separate the grains. Add the remaining salt and scallions and the shrimp mixture. Stir well and heat until the rice is piping hot. Garnish with chopped scallions.

Long-Grain and Wild Rice Ring

This side dish combines two types of rice with currants and onion, to give an unusual texture and delicious flavor.

Serves 8

INGREDIENTS

2 tablespoons corn oil, plus extra for
    greasing mold
1 large onion, chopped
2 cups mixed long-grain and wild rice
5 cups chicken stock
1/3 cup currants
salt
6 scallions, cut diagonally into
    1/4-inch pieces
fresh parsley sprigs, to garnish

corn oil

scallions

chicken stock

onion

parsley

mixed long-grain and wild rice

currants

1 Lightly oil a 7½-cup ring mold. Set aside. Heat the oil in a large saucepan. Add the onion and cook for 5 minutes, or until softened.

2 Add the rice to the pan and stir well to coat the rice with the oil.

3 Stir in the chicken stock and bring to a boil. Reduce the heat to low. Stir the currants into the rice mixture. Add salt to taste. Cover and simmer until the rice is tender and the stock has been absorbed, about 35 minutes. Drain the rice if necessary and transfer it to a mixing bowl. Stir in the scallions.

4 Pack the rice mixture into the prepared mold. Turn it out onto a warmed serving platter. Place parsley sprigs in the center of the ring before serving.

COOK'S TIP

Wild rice needs quite a lengthy cooking time, so you will need a particularly large amount of water to boil it in. It will, however, need a shorter cooking time if mixed with a long-grain rice. Wild rice is ready when the grains have begun to burst open, releasing their nutty aroma.

Okra Fried Rice

If you like hot food, you'll love this spicy Caribbean vegetable speciality.

Serves 3-4

INGREDIENTS
5 ounces okra
2 tablespoons oil
1 tablespoon butter or margarine
1 garlic clove, crushed
$\frac{1}{2}$ red onion, finely chopped
2 tablespoons diced green and red
    bell peppers
$\frac{1}{2}$ teaspoon dried thyme
2 green chiles, finely chopped
$\frac{1}{2}$ teaspoon five-spice powder
$\frac{1}{2}$ vegetable bouillon cube
2 tablespoons soy sauce
1 tablespoon chopped cilantro
scant 1 cup long-grain rice, cooked
freshly ground black pepper
cilantro sprigs, to garnish

oil

butter

red onion

green and red bell peppers

bouillon cube

garlic

thyme

okra

green chiles

five-spice powder

soy sauce

cilantro

long-grain rice

1 Wash and dry the okra, trim it and slice it thinly on a diagonal. Set aside until needed.

2 Heat the oil and butter or margarine in a frying pan or wok, add the garlic and onion and cook over moderate heat for 5 minutes, until soft. Add the sliced okra and sauté gently for 6–7 minutes.

3 Add the peppers, thyme, chiles and five-spice powder and cook for 3 minutes.

4 Crumble in the bouillon cube, add the soy sauce, chopped cilantro and rice and toss over the heat until the rice is piping hot. Add some freshly ground pepper. Serve, garnished with cilantro sprigs.

Rice Pilaf Flavored with Whole Spices

This fragrant rice dish will make a perfect accompaniment to any Indian meal.

Serves 4-6

INGREDIENTS
generous pinch of saffron strands
2½ cups hot chicken stock
4 tablespoons butter
1 onion, chopped
1 garlic clove, crushed
½ cinnamon stick
6 green cardamom pods
1 bay leaf
1⅓ cup basmati rice, rinsed and drained
⅓ cup golden raisins
1 tablespoon oil
½ cup cashew nuts

1 Add the saffron strands to the hot stock and set aside. Heat the butter in a large saucepan and cook the onion and garlic for 5 minutes. Stir in the cinnamon stick, cardamom and bay leaf and cook for 2 minutes.

saffron

chicken stock

cinnamon stick

onion

bay leaf

butter

oil

garlic

golden raisins

cardamom pods

basmati rice

cashew nuts

2 Add the rice and cook, stirring, for 2 minutes more. Pour in the stock and saffron mixture and add the raisins. Bring to a boil, stir, then lower the heat. Cover the pan and let cook gently for about 15 minutes, or until the rice is tender and all the liquid has been absorbed.

3 Meanwhile, heat the oil in a wok or frying pan and fry the cashew nuts until browned. Drain on paper towels. Sprinkle over the rice and serve.

VARIATION

You can add a mixture of nuts to this recipe, if you like, such as almonds, peanuts or hazelnuts. Some nuts may be bought complete with their brown, papery skins, which should be removed before use. The flavor of all nuts is improved by toasting.

COOK'S TIP

Remember to keep all spices stored in separate airtight containers. This helps them retain their flavor as well as preventing their aromas from spreading to other ingredients in your cupboard.

Mexican-style Rice

This side dish is the perfect accompaniment for chicken fajitas or flour tortillas. It is garnished with a stunning but dangerous display of flowers made from red chiles.

Serves 6

INGREDIENTS

1³/₄ cups long-grain rice
1 onion, chopped
2 garlic cloves, chopped
1 pound tomatoes, peeled, seeded and coarsely chopped
4 tablespoons corn or peanut oil
3³/₄ cups chicken stock
1¹/₂ cups peas, thawed if frozen
salt and freshly ground black pepper
cilantro sprigs and 4-6 red chile flowers, to garnish

long-grain rice *garlic* *onion* *tomatoes* *corn oil* *chicken stock* *cilantro* *red chiles* *peas*

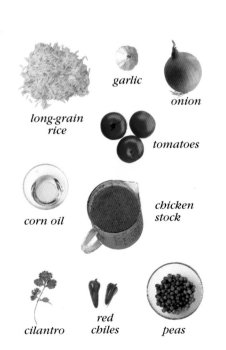

1 Soak the rice in a bowl of hot water for 15 minutes. Drain, rinse well under cold running water, drain again and set aside. Combine the onion, garlic and tomatoes in a food processor and process to a purée.

2 Heat the oil in a large frying pan. Add the drained rice and sauté until it becomes golden brown. Using a slotted spoon to leave behind as much oil as possible, transfer the rice to a saucepan.

COOK'S TIP

When making chile flowers, it is a good idea to wear rubber gloves and avoid touching your face or eyes, as the essential oils will cause a painful reaction. Slice the chiles from tip to stem end into four or five sections. Place in a bowl of ice water until they curl back to form flowers, then drain. Wash hands or gloves thoroughly.

3 Reheat the oil remaining in the pan and cook the tomato, garlic and onion purée for 2–3 minutes. Put it in the saucepan of rice and pour in the stock. Season to taste. Bring to a boil, reduce the heat to the lowest possible setting, cover the pan and cook for 15–20 minutes, until almost all the liquid has been absorbed.

4 Stir the peas into the rice mixture and cook, uncovered, until all the liquid has been absorbed and the rice is tender. Stir the mixture from time to time. Transfer the rice to a serving dish and garnish with the drained chile flowers and sprigs of cilantro. Warn the diners that the chile flowers are hot and should be approached with caution.

Rice Flavored with Saffron and Cardamom

This rice is delicately flavored with three aromatic spices to create a superb side dish. Serve it as an accompaniment to your favorite Indian curry.

Serves 6

INGREDIENTS
2¼ cups basmati rice
3 green cardamom pods
2 cloves
1 teaspoon salt
½ teaspoon crushed saffron strands
3 tablespoons milk

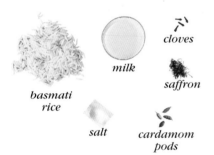

basmati rice *milk* *cloves* *saffron* *salt* *cardamom pods*

1 Wash the rice thoroughly, at least twice, drain and place in a saucepan with 3 cups of water.

2 Toss the cardamom and cloves into the saucepan along with the salt. Bring to a boil, cover, lower the heat and simmer for about 10 minutes. Meanwhile, place the saffron and milk in a small pan and warm.

COOK'S TIP

Saffron, the world's most expensive spice, is made from the stamen of the *Crocus sativus*. Two hundred thousand flowers are harvested by hand to obtain every pound saffron, which explains its high cost. It is appreciated for its delicate yet distinctive flavor and striking color, and is added to special dishes, savory as well as sweet, in many cuisines.

3 To see if the rice is fully cooked, use a slotted spoon to lift out a few grains and press the rice between your index finger and thumb. It should feel soft on the outside but still a little hard in the middle (al dente). Remove the pan from the heat and drain the rice through a sieve.

4 Pour the rice and whole spices back into the pan and spoon the saffron milk over the top.

5 Cover the pan with a tight-fitting lid and return to medium heat for 7–10 minutes. Remove the pan from the heat, leaving the lid on, and let the rice stand for 5 minutes before serving.

Tomato Rice

This vibrant rice dish owes its appeal as much to the bright colors of red onion, red bell pepper and cherry tomatoes as it does to their luscious, distinctive flavors.

Serves 2

INGREDIENTS
²/₃ cup basmati rice
2 tablespoons peanut oil
1 small red onion, chopped
1 red bell pepper, chopped
8 ounces cherry tomatoes, halved
2 eggs, beaten
salt and freshly ground black pepper
chopped fresh herbs, to garnish

eggs

peanut oil

red bell pepper

cherry tomatoes

red onion

mixed herbs

basmati rice

COOK'S TIP
Peanut oil has a very distinctive taste. Use it carefully at first, until you become used to the flavor. If you use peanut oil or any peanut product, always check that none of your guests are allergic to peanuts. Use corn oil instead, if you like.

1 Wash the rice several times under cold running water. Drain well. Bring a large pan of water to a boil, add the rice and cook for 10–12 minutes.

2 Meanwhile, heat the oil in a wok until very hot. Add the onion and pepper and stir-fry for 2–3 minutes. Add the cherry tomatoes and stir-fry for 2 minutes. Pour in the beaten eggs all at once.

3 Cook for 30 seconds without stirring, then stir to break up the eggs as they begin to set.

4 Drain the cooked rice thoroughly, add to the wok and toss it over the heat with the vegetable and egg mixture for 3 minutes. Season to taste. Garnish with chopped herbs.

Pigeon Peas Cook-up Rice

This African-style rice dish is made with the country's most commonly used peas. It is flavored with creamed coconut.

Serves 4-6

INGREDIENTS
2 tablespoons butter or margarine
1 onion, chopped
1 garlic clove, crushed
2 tablespoons chopped scallions
1 large carrot, diced
about 1 cup pigeon peas
1 fresh thyme sprig or 1 teaspoon
    dried thyme
1 cinnamon stick
2½ cups vegetable stock
4 tablespoons creamed coconut or
    coconut cream (unsweetened)
1 red chile, chopped
2¼ cups long-grain rice
salt and freshly ground black pepper

1 Melt the butter or margarine in a large, heavy saucepan, add the chopped onion and crushed garlic and sauté over medium heat for about 5 minutes, stirring occasionally.

 butter

 onion

 cinnamon

scallion

garlic *carrot* *chile*

 vegetable stock

long-grain rice

 creamed coconut

thyme

COOK'S TIP

Pigeon peas are also known as Congo peas. The fresh peas can be difficult to obtain, but you will find them in specialty shops. Drain the salted water from canned peas and rinse before using them in this recipe.

2 Add the scallions, carrot, pigeon peas, thyme, cinnamon, stock, creamed coconut or coconut cream, chile and seasoning. Bring to a boil.

3 Reduce the heat and stir in the rice. Cover and simmer over low heat for 10–15 minutes, or until all the liquid has been absorbed and the rice is tender. Stir with a fork to fluff up the rice before serving.

Rice Cakes with Cream and Mixed Mushrooms

Serve with rich meat dishes, such as beef stroganoff or goulash, or as part of a vegetarian supper menu.

Serves 4

INGREDIENTS

¾ cup long-grain rice
1 egg
1 tablespoon all-purpose flour
4 tablespoons freshly grated
   Parmesan, Fontina or Pecorino
   cheese
4 tablespoons unsalted butter, plus
   extra for frying rice cakes
1 small onion, chopped
1½-2 cups assorted wild and
   cultivated mushrooms, trimmed
   and sliced
1 fresh thyme sprig
2 tablespoons Madeira or sherry
⅔ cup sour cream or crème fraîche
salt and freshly ground black pepper
paprika for dusting (optional)

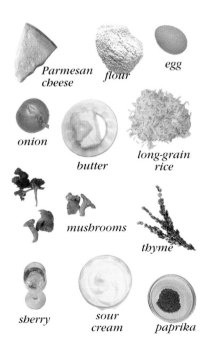

Parmesan cheese   flour   egg

onion   butter   long-grain rice

mushrooms   thyme

sherry   sour cream   paprika

1 Bring a saucepan of water to a boil. Add the rice and cook for about 12 minutes. Rinse, drain and cool.

2 Beat the egg, flour and cheese together with a fork, then stir in the cooled cooked rice. Mix well and set aside. Melt half the butter and cook the onion until soft but not browned. Add the mushrooms and thyme and cook until the juices run. Add the Madeira or sherry. Increase the heat to reduce the juices and concentrate the flavor. Season to taste, transfer to a bowl, cover and keep hot.

3 Using a tablespoon, shape the rice mixture into cakes. Melt a pat of butter in a frying pan and fry the rice cakes in batches for 1 minute on each side. Add more butter as needed. Keep the cooked rice cakes hot.

4 When all the rice cakes are cooked, arrange on four warmed plates, top with sour cream or crème fraîche and add a spoonful of mushrooms. Dust with paprika, if using. Serve with a selection of cooked vegetables, if you like.

COOK'S TIP

Although the recipe specifies Parmesan, Fontina or Pecorino, you could use aged Cheddar cheese or even a hard goat cheese.

Rice and Vegetable Stir-Fry

If you have some leftover cooked rice and a few vegetables to spare, then you've got the basis for this quick and tasty side dish.

Serves 4

INGREDIENTS

$^1/_2$ cucumber
1 small red or yellow bell pepper
2 carrots
3 tablespoons sunflower or peanut oil
2 scallions, sliced
1 garlic clove, crushed
$^1/_4$ small green cabbage, shredded
scant $^1/_2$ cup cup long-grain rice,
    cooked
2 tablespoons light soy sauce
1 tablespoon sesame oil
fresh parsley or cilantro, chopped
    (optional)
1 cup unsalted cashew nuts, almonds
    or peanuts
salt and freshly ground black pepper

cucumber

scallions

carrots

garlic

pepper

green
cabbage

soy
sauce

long-grain
rice

sunflower oil

parsley

sesame oil

cashew
nuts

1 Halve the cucumber lengthwise and scoop out the seeds with a teaspoon. Slice the flesh diagonally. Set aside.

2 Cut the red or yellow pepper in half and remove the core and seeds. Slice the pepper thinly.

3 Peel the carrots and cut into thin slices. Heat the oil in a wok or large frying pan and stir-fry the sliced scallions, garlic, carrots and pepper for 3 minutes, until the vegetables are crisp but still tender.

4 Add the cabbage and cucumber and cook for another minute or two, until the leaves begin to wilt. Mix in the rice, soy sauce, sesame oil and seasoning. Reheat the mixture thoroughly, stirring and tossing all the time. Add the herbs, if using, and nuts. Check the seasoning and adjust if necessary. Serve piping hot.

DESSERTS

Sticky Rice with Tropical Fruit Topping

A popular dessert. Mangoes, with their delicate fragrance, sweet and sour flavor and velvety flesh, blend especially well with coconut sticky rice. You need to start preparing this dish the day before.

Serves 4

INGREDIENTS
²/₃ cup glutinous (sticky) rice
³/₄ cup thick coconut milk
3 tablespoons sugar
pinch of salt
2 ripe mangoes
strips of lime zest, to decorate

glutinous rice

coconut milk

sugar

mangoes

lime

1 Rinse the glutinous rice thoroughly in several changes of cold water, then let soak overnight in a bowl of fresh, cold water. Drain and spread the rice in an even layer in a steamer lined with cheesecloth. Cover and steam for about 20 minutes, or until the grains of rice are tender.

2 Meanwhile, reserve 3 tablespoons of the top of the coconut milk and combine the rest with the sugar and salt in a saucepan. Bring to a boil, stirring until the sugar dissolves, then pour into a bowl and let cool a little. Turn the rice out into a bowl and pour the coconut mixture over it. Stir, then set aside for 10–15 minutes.

3 Peel the mangoes and cut the flesh into slices. Place on top of the rice and drizzle with the reserved coconut milk. Decorate with strips of lime zest.

VARIATION
If mangoes are not available, top the sticky rice pudding with a compote made by poaching dried apricots in water to cover for about 15 minutes.

Caramel Rice

Indulge in this version of the classic sweet rice dish, which is particularly delicious when served with fresh fruit.

Serves 4

INGREDIENTS
1/3 cup short-grain rice
5 tablespoons demerara or
    brown sugar
pinch of salt
14-ounce can evaporated milk
    with enough water added
    to make 2 1/2 cups
pat of butter
1 small fresh pineapple
2 crisp apples
2 teaspoons lemon juice

short-grain rice

lemon

apples

pineapple

demerara sugar

butter

evaporated milk

1 Preheat the oven to 300°F. Put the rice in a sieve and wash under cold running water. Drain well and put into a lightly greased soufflé dish. Add 2 tablespoons of the sugar and the salt to the dish. Pour in the diluted evaporated milk and stir gently. Dot the surface of the rice with butter. Bake for 2 hours, then set aside to cool for about 30 minutes.

COOK'S TIP

Rice pudding is a popular dessert in many different countries, so the possibilities for making different variations are endless. You can try sprinkling grated nutmeg on top instead of sugar, or decorate it with chopped almonds, pistachios and ground cinnamon. Rice pudding is also delicious chilled.

2 Meanwhile, peel, core and slice the pineapple and apples, then cut the pineapple into chunks. Toss the fruit in the lemon juice and set aside.

3 Preheat the broiler and sprinkle the remaining sugar over the rice pudding. Broil for 5 minutes, until the sugar has caramelized. Let the rice stand for 5 minutes to allow the caramel to harden, then serve with the fresh fruit.

Fragrant Rice Pudding with Mango Purée

Nuts, dried fruit, cardamom and rose water make this Indian-style rice pudding a real treat.

Serves 6

INGREDIENTS
2 ripe mangoes
scant $\frac{1}{3}$ cup basmati rice
$6\frac{1}{4}$ cups milk
$\frac{1}{4}$ cup demerara or brown sugar
$\frac{1}{3}$ cup golden raisins
1 teaspoon rose water
5 green cardamom pods
3 tablespoons orange juice
3 tablespoons sliced almonds, toasted
3 tablespoons pistachio nuts, chopped

mangoes

golden raisins

basmati rice

milk

demerara sugar

orange juice

sliced almonds

pistachio nuts

cardamom

1 Using a sharp knife, peel, slice and pit the mangoes.

2 Preheat the oven to 300°F. Put the basmati rice in an ovenproof dish. Bring the milk to a boil in a saucepan, then pour it over the rice. Bake, uncovered, for 2 hours, until the rice has become soft and mushy.

3 Remove the dish from the oven and stir in the sugar and raisins, with half the rose water. Crush the cardamom pods, extract the seeds and stir them into the rice mixture. Set aside to cool.

4 Place the mango flesh in a blender or food processor. Add the orange juice and remaining rose water. Blend until smooth. Divide the mango purée among six individual glass serving dishes. Spoon the rice pudding mixture evenly over the top. Let chill thoroughly in the refrigerator. When ready to serve, sprinkle the toasted almonds and chopped pistachio nuts over the top of each pudding.

VARIATION
Make this nutritious dessert an even healthier option by decorating it with slices of fruit instead of nuts.

Mexican Rice Pudding

Here is another delicious version of the classic rice dessert. This Mexican recipe—*arroz con leche*—is light and attractive and combines many tantalizing flavors. It is surprisingly easy to make.

Serves 4

INGREDIENTS
1/2 cup raisins
1/2 cup short-grain rice
1-inch strip of pared lime or lemon
    zest
2 cups milk
1 cup sugar
1/4 teaspoon salt
1-inch piece of cinnamon stick
2 egg yolks, well beaten
1 tablespoon unsalted butter, cubed
toasted sliced almonds to decorate
segments of fresh peeled oranges,
    to serve

raisins   short-grain   milk
              rice

cinnamon

lime   eggs   oranges

sugar   butter   sliced
                    almonds

1 Soak the raisins in warm water to cover until plump. Place the rice in a saucepan with 1 cup water and the citrus zest. Bring slowly to a boil, then cover and simmer for 20 minutes, until the water is absorbed.

2 Remove the zest from the rice and discard it. Add the milk, sugar, salt and cinnamon and cook, stirring, over very low heat until all the milk has been absorbed. Do not cover the pan.

3 Discard the cinnamon stick. Beat in the egg yolks. Drain the raisins well and stir them into the rice. Add the cubed butter and stir until it has melted and the pudding is rich and creamy. Cook for a few minutes longer.

4 Scrape the pudding into a dish and let cool. Decorate with the almonds and serve with the orange segments.

Rice Pudding with Mixed Berry Sauce

An irresistible combination of creamy rice with refreshing summer fruits that gives a new meaning to the phrase "comfort food."

Serves 6

INGREDIENTS
2 cups short-grain rice
1¼ cups milk
pinch of salt
⅔ cup soft light brown sugar
1 teaspoon vanilla extract
2 eggs, beaten
grated zest of 1 lemon
1 teaspoon fresh lemon juice
2 tablespoons butter or margarine
strawberry leaves, to decorate
    (optional)

FOR THE SAUCE
6 ounces (1¼ cups) strawberries,
    hulled and quartered
1½ cups raspberries
½ cup granulated sugar
grated zest of 1 lemon

short-grain rice
vanilla extract
eggs
lemon
milk
brown sugar
butter
raspberries
strawberries
sugar

1 Preheat the oven to 325°F. Grease a 4-cup baking dish. Bring a saucepan of water to a boil. Add the rice and boil for 5 minutes. Drain. Transfer the rice to the prepared baking dish.

2 In a bowl, combine the milk, salt, brown sugar, vanilla, egg, and lemon zest and juice. Pour this mixture over the rice and stir well. Dot the surface of the rice mixture with the butter or margarine. Bake for about 50 minutes, until the rice is cooked and creamy.

3 Meanwhile, make the sauce. Mix the berries and granulated sugar in a small saucepan. Stir over low heat until the sugar has dissolved completely and the fruit is becoming pulpy. Transfer to a bowl and stir in the lemon zest. Chill the sauce until required.

4 Remove the rice pudding from the oven. Let cool completely, and serve with the berry sauce. Decorate with strawberry leaves, if you like.

Thai-style Dessert

Black glutinous rice, also known as black sticky rice, makes a tasty pudding. It tastes nutty, rather like wild rice.

Serves 4-6

INGREDIENTS
scant 1 cup black glutinous (sticky) rice
2 tablespoons light brown sugar
2 cups coconut milk
3 eggs
2 tablespoons granulated sugar

light brown sugar

coconut milk

eggs

black glutinous rice

granulated sugar

1 Combine the glutinous rice, brown sugar, half the coconut milk and 1 cup of water in a saucepan. Bring to a boil, then simmer, stirring from time to time, for 15–20 minutes, or until the rice has absorbed most of the liquid. Preheat the oven to 300°F.

3 Place the dish or ramekins in a baking pan. Pour in enough boiling water to come halfway up the sides of the dish or ramekins. Cover with foil and bake for 35 minutes to 1 hour, or until the custard is set. Serve warm or cold, whichever you prefer.

2 Transfer the rice to one large ovenproof dish or divide it among individual ramekins. Mix the eggs, remaining coconut milk and granulated sugar in a bowl. Strain and pour the mixture evenly over the rice mixture.

VARIATION
Black glutinous rice is popular in Southeast Asia for sweet dishes. Its character contributes to the delicious flavor of this dessert. Use white glutinous rice if the black grain is difficult to find.

COOK'S TIP
A pan of water in which dishes of delicate food are cooked is known as a bain-marie.

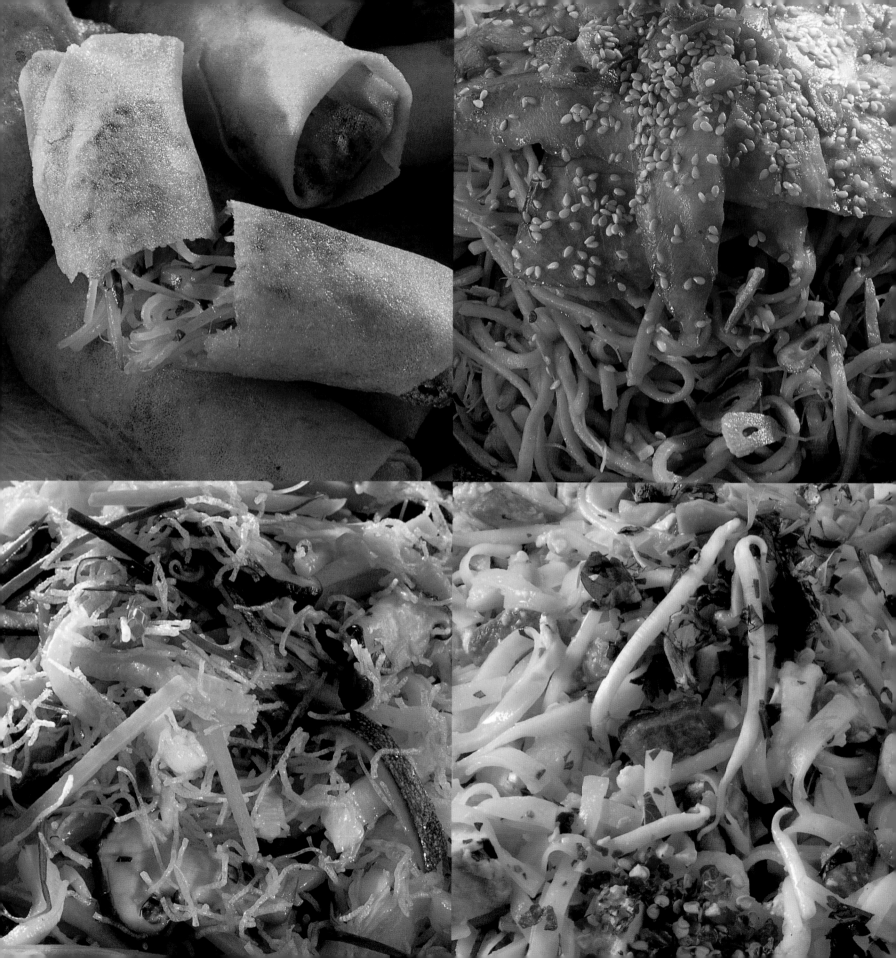

noodles

INTRODUCING NOODLES

Noodles are loved the world over and are used in countless recipes. Thanks to Marco Polo, noodles have an undisputed place in Western kitchens, but this section concentrates on the noodle dishes of Asia. China, Thailand, Japan and Indonesia, together with Vietnam, Burma (now called Myanmar) and Malaysia, have their own traditional noodle dishes, and many of these have become as popular in the West as they are in their own countries. Chow Mein, Singapore Noodles, Thai Fried Noodles and Japanese Chilled Noodles with Dashi Dip are now among our own favorites and are just a few of the many superb dishes featured in this section.

Unlike Italian pasta, which is produced almost exclusively from wheat, Asian noodles are also made from rice, bean starch and even from arrowroot, generally depending on the principal crop of the region. Wheat noodles are one of the staple foods of northern China, where wheat is the primary grain. These are made with or without egg and are sold in a huge variety of widths, from fine vermicelli strands to thick broad ribbons. Rice noodles, characterized by their opaque, pale color, also come in a range of widths, while cellophane noodles (made from ground mung beans) are thin and wiry, used for soups or adding to vegetable dishes.

In many cuisines, noodles play an important role in traditional festivities. In China they are a symbol of longevity, eaten at birthdays and weddings and as "crossing of the threshold of the year" food. They are also a favorite snack food, sold on the street, tossed simply with flavored oils, garlic or ginger or served with meat and vegetables. Noodles are the original fast food in the East, sold everywhere and for everyone at any time of the day. This section offers a selection of all types of noodle dishes, from soups and snacks to main dishes for the family and for special occasions.

Types of Noodles

The range of Asian noodles is extensive, from fine and thin to coarse and thick, made of wheat flour (with or without egg), rice flour or vegetable starch, and available fresh or dried. They are amazingly versatile.

Chinese noodles

Depending on the region and therefore on locally grown produce, Chinese noodles are made from one of three main ingredients—wheat flour, rice flour or mung beans. They come in a variety of shapes and thicknesses, often tied into bundles with raffia, or coiled into squares or oblongs. They are traditionally long, as this is believed to symbolize a long life.

Although most Southeast Asian countries produce their own noodles, Chinese-style noodles can be used for any of the dishes from Malaysia, Indonesia and Thailand. Like pasta, most noodles are interchangeable, and if a certain type or thickness of noodle isn't available, a similar one can be used instead. The exception is cellophane noodles, which are used more as a vegetable to give texture to a dish, than as a staple.

Wheat noodles

These come from northern China, where wheat is the principal grain. Pure wheat noodles are often packaged like Italian spaghetti, in long thin sticks, or wound into nests.

Egg noodles

Egg noodles are the most common and most versatile of all Chinese noodles. They are made from wheat with egg added, giving the characteristic yellow color. Fresh egg noodles, which are becoming increasingly available—not only in Chinese stores, but also in most large supermarkets—are usually sold in thick coils and resemble loosely tangled balls of wool.

Dried egg noodles are normally coiled into compressed squares or oblongs. They come in a variety of thicknesses, from thin, threadlike noodles to broad, thick strips, and they can be ribbon-shaped or rounded.

Fresh noodles, like fresh pasta, have a better flavor and texture, but for cooking times check the package instructions, as these will depend on their thickness. Dried noodles are best soaked briefly in warm water to untangle before adding to your dish.

Cellophane or mung bean noodles

These are made from ground mung beans and are also known as bean threads or transparent noodles. They are thin and wiry and sold in bundles tied with a thread, but unlike rice vermicelli, they are translucent and are not brittle, and can only be broken up using scissors.

The dried noodles need to be soaked before cooking, and then can be used in soups and other dishes with plenty of sauce or stock, as they absorb four times their weight in liquid.

In a continent where texture is as important as flavor, these slippery-textured noodles are very popular, and while they have little or no flavor of their own, they will take on the flavors of other ingredients.

Rice noodles

Made from ground rice, these come from southern parts of China, where rice is the staple crop. They range in thickness from very thin to wide ribbons and sheets. Dried ribbon rice noodles are usually sold tied together in bundles or come coiled into square packages.

Rice vermicelli

Made from rice flour, these noodles are very thin, white and brittle and are sold in large bundles, often tied with cotton string or raffia. They should be soaked briefly and will then cook almost instantly in hot liquid. In their dried form they can be deep-fried for crisp noodles—don't soak them first.

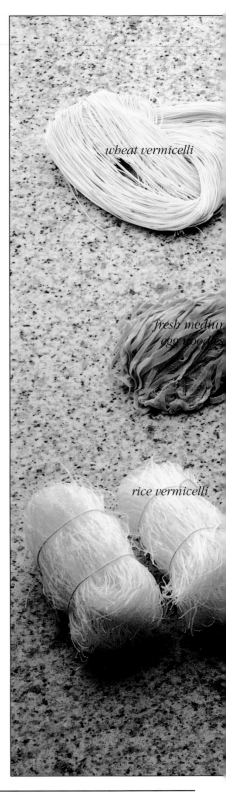

wheat vermicelli

fresh medium egg noodles

rice vermicelli

wheat noodles

chow mein

wheat wonton wrapper

fresh Shanghai noodles

fresh fine egg noodles

dried egg noodles

egg wonton wrapper

rice sheets

fresh rice noodles

dried cellophane noodles

Japanese noodles

There are four main types of Japanese noodle, all of which play an important part in Japanese cuisine. Although distinct from Chinese noodles, they share many of the same characteristics. Most Japanese noodles are available at Chinese markets; they are as popular in Chinese cuisine as they are in Japanese.

Gyoza wrappers

The Japanese equivalent of wonton skins. The wrappers can be filled with ground meat, fish, vegetables and seasonings. They are usually browned on one side, turned and simmered in broth and served as appetizers.

Harusame noodles

Meaning "spring rain," these transparent noodles are the equivalent of Chinese cellophane noodles. They can be deep-fried or soaked and are used in a variety of dishes.

Soba noodles

Made from a mixture of buckwheat and wheat flour, these noodles are very popular in Japan. Thin and brownish in color, they are used in soups and are sometimes served cold with garnishes and a dipping sauce. They are best cooked in simmering water for a few minutes, until tender.

Somen noodles

These are very fine, white noodles made from wheat flour. They come dried, usually tied in bundles, held together with a paper band.

They are ideal in soups and in the popular Japanese one-pot meals and are also often served cold as a summer dish. If they are not available, vermicelli pasta can be used instead.

Udon noodles

These are the most popular and versatile of Japanese noodles. Like somen noodles, they are made from white wheat flour, but they are thicker and more substantial. They are normally rounded in shape like spaghetti, although they can be flat.

Udon noodles are available fresh, precooked or dried. Fresh noodles need only a few minutes' cooking in simmering water. For noodles straight from the package, follow the directions provided. Udon noodles are generally served in hot soups and in mixed meat and vegetable dishes.

Other noodles:
River rice noodles

Made from rice ground with water, these Chinese noodles have been steamed into thin sheets before being cut into ribbons about $1/2$ inch wide. They can be used in stir-fries or chow mein dishes. If possible, buy fresh noodles, as they have an excellent flavor and texture. Dried noodles should be boiled and drained before use.

Spring roll wrappers

Thinner and larger than wonton wrappers, these are made from wheat flour and water. There are two types, the Cantonese, which are smooth, like a noodle dough, and the Shanghai, which are transparent, like rice paper.

Wonton wrappers

These are made from the same dough as egg noodles, namely wheat flour, egg and water, cut into circles and 3-inch squares of varying thicknesses. They are normally sold fresh or frozen; if frozen, they will keep for several months.

NOODLE KNOW-HOW

Dried noodles should be stored in airtight containers, where they can be kept for many months. Fresh noodles will keep in the refrigerator for 3–4 days, or in an unopened package until their use-by date. They can also be frozen for up to 6 months.

Quantities will depend not only on appetite but also on whether there are accompanying noodle or rice dishes. If noodles are the principal dish, allow 3–4 ounces fresh noodles or one square or oblong of dried noodles per person. The exception is cellophane noodles, which are used more as a vegetable and therefore quantities will generally be smaller. Cellophane noodles may need presoaking for 30 minutes.

Gyoza wrappers

somen noodles

Fresh and Pantry Essentials

Almost all ingredients you can think of—and many you wouldn't—can be used in noodle dishes. Many of the traditional Asian ingredients are available in supermarkets or in Asian markets, so it is possible to make dishes from the East that are absolutely authentic.

Bamboo shoots

These are available fresh but are more commonly seen canned. They have a fairly bland flavor and are generally used for their crunchy texture. Drain well and rinse under cold water before using in a recipe.

Bean curd/Tofu

This soybean product is available in several forms, including soft, firm, silken and dried. Plain, uncooked bean curd is entirely neutral in taste, absorbing the flavor of other ingredients.

It is low in fat, high in protein and calcium, and is therefore a versatile and useful ingredient for healthy, low-calorie meals.

Bean curd cheese/ Red fermented bean curd

This deep red bean curd has a very strong and cheesy flavor. It is fermented with salt, red rice and rice wine and is used in Asian cooking for flavoring meat, poultry and vegetarian dishes. It is usually stored in jars or earthenware pots and will keep for several months if refrigerated.

Bean sprouts

Used for their delicious texture in meat and vegetable dishes, bean sprouts are cooked for only 30 seconds. They will keep for 1–2 days in the refrigerator, but will discolor and wilt if left any longer.

Bok choy

This attractive, cabbagelike vegetable has a long, smooth, milky-white stem and large, dark green leaves.

Bonito

In Japanese cookery, these are dried flakes of a strongly flavored tuna. They are used frequently for stocks and soups and can be sprinkled over food as a seasoning.

Chinese cabbage

The crisp leaves of this vegetable (there are several types) are ideal for stir-frying or for soups. They are particularly popular in the latter, where their crunchy texture contrasts wonderfully with cellophane noodles.

Chinese mushrooms

These add flavor and texture to numerous Asian dishes. They are almost always sold dried and should be soaked before using. The caps are then sliced or halved, the stems discarded.

Cloud ears

These Chinese mushrooms are only available dried. After soaking they expand to form thick, brown clusters. They have little or no flavor, absorbing flavors from other seasonings, but are appreciated for their silky but crunchy texture. Rinse well to remove any sand and discard any hard bits.

Coconut milk/ Coconut cream

Used in almost all Asian cuisine, coconut milk is especially popular in Thai, Indonesian and Malaysian cooking, where it is used extensively, particularly in fish and poultry dishes.

Cans of coconut milk and cream are available from most supermarkets, as well as Asian stores. Buy unsweetened coconut milk. If the recipe calls for sugar, add this yourself.

Creamed coconut is a solid white block of coconut oil and other fats. It may not be available; coconut cream can be substituted, though the results will not be the same.

Daikon

Also known as mooli or Chinese radish, this large, white vegetable has a smooth, creamy-white skin and is normally sold with feathery, green tops. It has a pleasant, slightly spicy taste and is excellent steamed, pickled, used in stir-fries and chow mein or thinly sliced and eaten raw.

Dashi

The name given to the Japanese kombu and bonito stock. Instant dashi is available at Japanese and most large Chinese grocers.

Enoki mushrooms

These small cultivated mushrooms have long, thin stems and tiny, white caps. They are harvested in clumps attached at the base, which should be cut off before use. They have a crisp texture and delicate flavor and may be eaten raw or lightly cooked. When using in cooked dishes, add at the last minute, as heating tends to toughen them.

Fermented black beans

These whole soy beans are preserved in salt and ginger. They are pungent in taste, but when cooked in stir-fries or other dishes with additional ingredients bring a delicious flavor to the meal.

Fish sauce

This is an essential ingredient in many Southeast Asian countries, particularly Thailand and Indonesia.

Made from the liquid from salted fermented fish, it has a strong aroma and taste. Use sparingly until you acquire the taste.

Kombu

This popular Japanese ingredient is a type of kelp (seaweed) and is used to flavor stock. Kombu and bonito flake stock granules are available at Japanese markets, as is a liquid form and a tea bag–style instant stock. Kombu can also be served as a vegetable.

Mustard greens/ Mustard cabbage

There are many varieties of mustard greens, but the most commonly available and most suitable for cooking, rather than pickling, are those with a pale green stalk and large, single, oval leaf. They have a very distinctive taste and are used in soups and thick stews.

Nori/Yakinori/Ao-nori

Nori is dried seaweed, popular in Japanese and some Thai cooking. It is sold in paper-thin sheets that are dark green to black in color. It is normally toasted and used as a wrapping for sushi and as a garnish.

Yakinori are toasted sheets and ao-nori is a flaked, dried green seaweed used for seasoning. Both are available at Asian markets.

Oil

The favorite oil in most Asian cooking is peanut oil. It has a rich, nutty flavor. However, corn oil or sunflower oil can be used as a satisfactory substitute.

Asian sesame oil, with its distinct, nutty flavor, is made from toasted sesame seeds and is used for stirring into noodles

Right: Just some of the fresh ingredients used in Asian cooking available at large supermarkets.

or sprinkling over noodle dishes. It burns easily and is not recommended for cooking; however, a little will add a wonderful, aromatic flavor.

Rice vinegar

This is a pale vinegar with a distinct but delicate flavor. It is milder than most other light wine vinegars and is available at Asian stores.

Rice wine

Chinese rice wine has a rich, sherrylike flavor and is used in marinades or added to stir-fries or fried noodle dishes. It is available at most large supermarkets and Asian grocers.

Sake

This Japanese rice wine is now widely available. It is used occasionally in marinades or at the end of cooking and is frequently served, either hot or chilled, with Japanese meals.

Shiitake mushrooms

These tasty, firm-textured Japanese mushrooms are available fresh or dried. They have a meaty, slightly acidic flavor and a rather slippery texture. Dried mushrooms should be soaked in hot water for about 20 minutes and then strained. Save the water for the sauce. Add to stir-fries for a delicious flavor and texture.

Wood ears

These are similar to cloud ears, though larger in size and coarser in texture. Mild in flavor, they absorb the taste of more strongly flavored ingredients and are used mainly in soups and stir-fries, adding texture and color.

Yard-long beans

These long, thin beans are closely related to black-eyed peas. They are three or four times longer than green beans. Cut into smaller lengths and use just like ordinary beans.

Available at most Asian stores, choose those that are small and flexible. They can be refrigerated for up to 5 days.

Herbs, Spices and Flavorings

Try to keep a selection of these ingredients handy, so that you can rustle up a quick and delicious noodle dish without extensive shopping.

Chiles

There is a wide range of fresh and dried chiles from which to choose. Generally the larger the chile, the milder the flavor, although there are exceptions, so be warned!

Chinese chives

Also known as garlic chives, these have larger leaves than ordinary chives and have a mild garlic flavor. They need very little cooking, so stir them into a dish just before serving or use raw as a garnish. Look for plump, uniformly green specimens with no brown spots.

Cilantro

Cilantro (fresh coriander) has a distinct flavor, adding an essential pungency to many Chinese or Indonesian-style dishes. Finely or roughly chop and add to a dish just before serving, or use as a garnish. Bunches of leaves will keep for up to 5 days in a jar of water.

Cumin

Available as whole seed or ground, cumin has a pungent flavor and is used widely in beef dishes and other dishes requiring a curry flavor. Store in a cool, dark place for no more than 6 months.

Dried shrimp

Not to be confused with our own shrimp, these are small, shelled shrimp that have been salted and dried in the sun. They have a strong, fishy taste and are used as a seasoning for meat and vegetables in Chinese, Thai and Indonesian cooking. Rinse under cold water before use.

Dried shrimp paste or Shrimp sauce

Made from ground shrimp fermented in brine, this has a strong aroma and flavor and is used in Chinese, Thai and Malaysian cuisine to enhance seafood dishes. It is usually sold in jars and will keep almost indefinitely in a cool place.

Five-spice powder

A pungent mixture of cloves, cinnamon, fennel, star anise and Szechuan pepper, used extensively in Chinese cooking.

Galangal

This rhizome is reminiscent of ginger, pine and citrus and is similar in appearance to ginger, except that it is thinner and the young shoots are bright pink.

Peel in the same way as fresh ginger root and add to sauces and curries. Remove from the dish before serving.

Ginger

This is an essential ingredient in Asian cooking, used for its warm, fresh flavor and pleasant spiciness. Fresh ginger root is widely available and cannot be replaced with ground ginger. Choose ginger with a firm, unblemished skin, peel with a sharp knife and then finely chop or grate according to the recipe.

Kaffir lime leaves

Also known simply as lime leaves, these add a unique flavor and are excellent in marinades as well as stir-fries and sauces. The leaves need to be bruised by rubbing between your fingers to release the flavor. If fresh leaves are not available, dried leaves can be used instead.

Lemongrass

This aromatic herb has a thin, tapering stem and a citrusy, verbena flavor. To use, thinly slice the bulb end of the root and add to marinades or sauces according to the recipe.

Mirin

Sweet cooking sake, this has a delicate flavor and is usually added in the final stages of cooking.

Seven-flavor spice or Shichimi

Used in Japanese cooking, this has a noticeably Asian tang. It is made of sansho, seaweed, chile, tangerine peel, poppy seeds and white and black sesame seeds.

Soy sauce

Made from fermented soybeans, together with salt, sugar and yeast, this is one of the most ancient and popular seasonings in Asian cooking. There are three main types: Chinese dark or thick soy sauce and light or thin soy sauce, and Japanese soy sauce.

Dark soy sauce, which gives a reddish-brown hue to food, is used for meaty "red-braised" dishes. Light soy sauce is thinner in consistency and paler in color. It still has a salty flavor, but is used for paler dishes, such as chicken or fish. Japanese soy sauce (also called shoyu) is lighter in flavor than Chinese soy sauces and is best used when making the more delicate Japanese food.

Star anise

This spice has a pungent, aniseed flavor and is used either ground or whole.

Szechuan chile paste/ Chile paste

This hot paste of dried red chiles and ground yellow bean sauce is wonderful in fish dishes.

Tamarind

The brown, sticky pulp of the beanlike seed pod of the tamarind tree. The pulp is usually diluted with water and strained before use. Tamarind has a sour, yet fruity taste, resembling sour prunes.

Right: Experiment with the wonderful array of Asian herbs and spices available today.

Equipment

You will find most of the cooking equipment you have around the kitchen will be all you need. A wok is probably the most useful item, although even that is not essential, as a large frying pan can be substituted. However, if you are interested in investing in authentic tools of the trade, consider some of the following:

Bamboo skewers
These are widely used for barbecues and broiled foods. They should be soaked before use, and then discarded afterward.

Chopping board
A good-quality chopping board with a thick surface is essential and will last for years.

Citrus zester
This tool is designed to remove the rind or zest of citrus fruit while leaving the bitter white pith. It can also be used for shaving fresh coconut.

Cleaver
The weight of the cleaver makes it ideal for chopping all kinds of ingredients. Keep it sharp.

Cooking chopsticks
These are extra-long and allow you to stir ingredients in the wok while keeping a safe distance.

Draining wire
This is designed to sit on the side of the wok and is used mainly for deep-frying.

Food processor
Useful for numerous kitchen tasks, this is a quick alternative to the mortar and pestle.

Knives
It is very important to use the right-sized knife for the job, both for safety and for efficiency. There are two essential knives that should be in every kitchen. A chopping knife with a heavy, wide blade about 7–8 inches long is ideal for chopping vegetables, meats and fresh herbs. A paring knife has a smaller blade and is necessary for trimming and peeling vegetables and fruits.

Ladle
A long-handled ladle is very useful for spooning out soups, stock and sauces.

Mortar and pestle
A deep granite mortar and pestle is ideal for crushing garlic, ginger and herbs to a paste or for grinding small amounts of spices.

Rice paddle
Used to fluff up rice after cooking.

Saucepan
A good saucepan with a tight-fitting lid is essential for cooking rice properly.

Sharpening stone
A traditional tool for sharpening knives and cleavers. It is available at hardware stores.

Stainless-steel skimmer
This can be used when strong flavors are likely to affect bare-metal cooking implements.

Wire skimmer
This is the Asian alternative to a slotted spoon, and one or the other is absolutely essential in Asian cooking. Use for removing cooked food from boiling water or hot fat. However, it should not be used with fish-based liquids, as the strong flavor is likely to react with the metal.

Wok
The shape of the wok allows ingredients to be cooked in a minimum of fat, thus retaining freshness and flavor. There are several varieties available, including the carbon steel and the round-bottomed or Pau wok. A round-bottomed wok is best suited to a gas stove, where you will be able to control the amount of heat needed more easily. The carbon-steel, flat-bottomed wok is best for electric or solid-fuel stoves as it gives a better heat distribution.

Warm the wok gently before adding the oil for cooking. The oil then floods easily over the warm pan and prevents food from sticking.

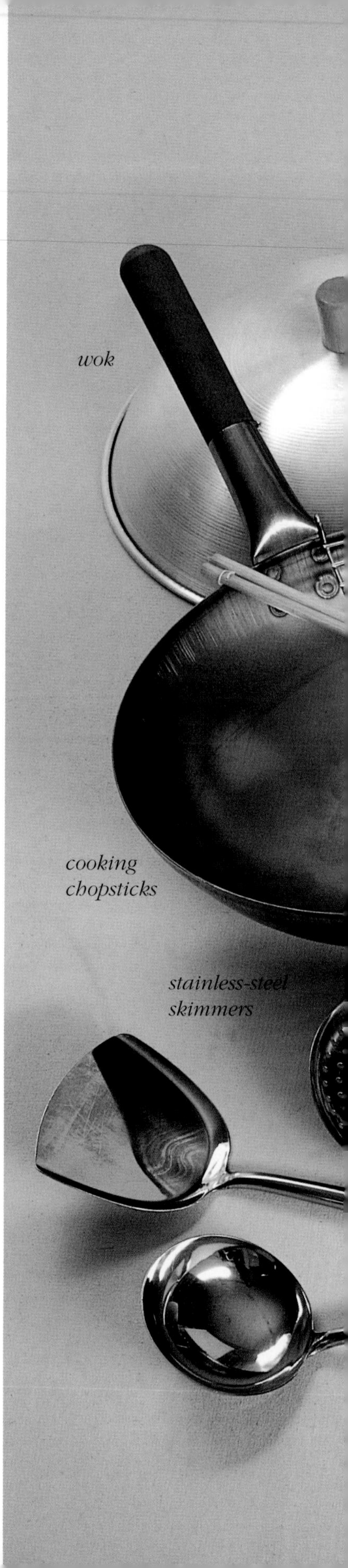

wok

cooking chopsticks

stainless-steel skimmers

food processor

bamboo skewers

saucepan

chopping
board

chopping
knife

draining
wire

sharpening
stone

citrus
zester

cleavers

mortar
and pestle

rice paddle

wire skimmer

Basic Techniques

Preparing Lemongrass

Use the whole stem and remove it before cooking, or chop the root.

1 Cut off and discard the dry, leafy tops. Peel away any tough outer layers. Trim off the tops and end of the stem until you are left with about 4 inches.

2 Lay the lemongrass on a board. Set the flat side of a chef's knife on top and strike it firmly with your fist. Cut across the lemongrass to make thin slices.

Preparing Kaffir Lime Leaves

The distinctive lime-lemon aroma and flavor of kaffir lime leaves are a vital part of Thai cooking.

COOK'S TIP

Buy fresh lime leaves at Asian stores and freeze them for future use. Dried lime leaves are also now available.

1 You can tear, shred or cut kaffir lime leaves. Using a small, sharp knife, carefully remove the center vein. Cut the leaves crosswise into very fine strips.

Preparing Fresh Ginger

Fresh ginger root can be used in slices, strips or finely chopped (or grated).

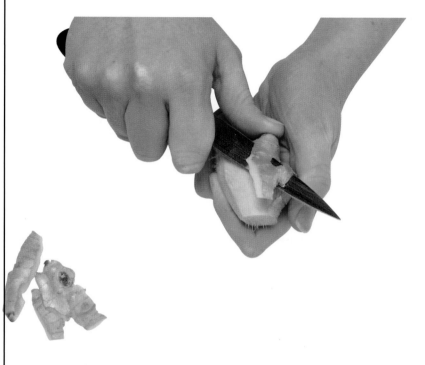

1 Using a small, sharp knife, peel the skin from the ginger root.

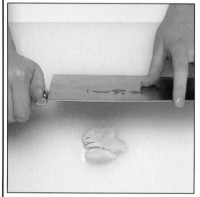

2 Place the ginger on a board, set the flat side of a cleaver or chef's knife on top and strike it firmly with your fist—this will soften the fiberous texture.

3 Chop the ginger as coarsely or finely as you wish, moving the blade backward and forward.

Preparing Bean Sprouts

Usually available at supermarkets, bean sprouts add a crisp texture to stir-fries.

1 Pick over the bean sprouts, discarding any pieces that are discolored, broken or wilted.

2 Rinse the bean sprouts under cold running water and drain well.

Preparing Scallions

Use scallions in stir-fries to flavor oil, as a vegetable in their own right or as a garnish.

1 Trim off the root and any discolored tops with a sharp knife. For an intense flavor in a stir-fry, cut the entire scallion into thin matchsticks.

2 Alternatively, slice the white and pale green part of the scallion diagonally and stir-fry with crushed garlic to flavor the cooking oil.

Chopping Cilantro

Chop cilantro just before you use it; the flavor will be much better.

1 Strip the leaves from the stalks and pile them on a chopping board.

2 Using a cleaver or chef's knife, cut the cilantro into small pieces, moving the blade back and forth until it is as coarsely or finely chopped as you wish.

Preparing Chiles

The flavor of chile is wonderful in cooking, but fresh chiles must be handled with care.

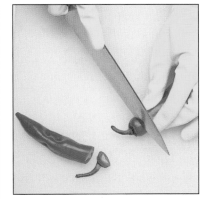

1 Wearing rubber gloves, remove the stalks from the chiles.

2 Cut in half lengthwise. Scrape out the seeds and fleshy, white ribs from each half, using a sharp knife. Chop or thinly slice according to the recipe.

Seasoning a Wok

If you are using a new wok or frying pan, you will need to prepare it as follows, to ensure the best results.

1 A brand-new wok will probably have been given a protective coating of oil by the manufacturer, which will need to be removed before seasoning. To do this, scrub the wok with a cream cleanser, rinse thoroughly and dry.

To season the wok, place it over low heat and add 2 tablespoons vegetable oil.

2 Using a pad of paper towels, rub the entire inside of the wok with the oil, then heat slowly for 10–15 minutes.

3 Alternatively, add 2–3 tablespoons salt to the wok and heat slowly for the same length of time.

4 Wipe the inside of the wok clean with more paper towels; the paper will become black. Repeat the process of coating, heating and wiping several times until the paper is no longer blackened. The wok is now seasoned and will have a good nonstick surface; do not scrub it again.

COOK'S TIP
To keep a seasoned wok clean, just wash it in hot water without detergent, then wipe it dry. The wok may rust if not in constant use. If it does, scour the rust off and repeat the seasoning process.

Deep-frying

The advantage of a wok is that it can be used for deep-frying as well as stir-frying. It uses far less oil than a deep fat fryer.

1 Put the wok on a stand and half-fill with oil. Heat until the required temperature registers on a thermometer. Alternatively, test by dropping in a small piece of food: If bubbles form all over the surface, the oil is ready.

2 Carefully add the food to the oil using long wooden chopsticks or tongs, and move it around to prevent it from sticking together. Using a bamboo strainer or slotted spoon, carefully remove the food and drain on paper towels before serving. Make sure that the wok is fully secure on its stand before adding the oil. Never leave the wok unattended.

Stir-frying

Many noodle recipes, such as chow mein, involve stir-frying. A wok is the perfect piece of equipment for this type of cooking.

1 Prepare all the ingredients before you start cooking, using a small, sharp knife to cut the vegetables into even-sized pieces. Meat should be cut into thin slices against the grain. It may be easier to slice meat if it has been frozen slightly for an hour or so beforehand. By the time you have sliced it, the meat will be ready to cook.

2 Make sure all the ingredients are close by, as wok cooking needs constant attention. Heat the wok for a few minutes before adding the oil.

3 When the pan is hot, add the oil and swirl it or brush it around to coat the bottom and sides of the wok. Allow the oil to heat for a few moments.

4 Reduce the heat a little as you add the first ingredients, to ensure that they do not burn and that aromatics, like garlic and scallions, do not become bitter. Stir-fry over quite a high heat, but not so high that food sticks and burns.

5 Foods should be added in a specific order, usually aromatics first (garlic, ginger, scallions), followed by the main ingredients that require some cooking, such as meats and denser vegetables and then the finer ingredients. Keep the ingredients moving in the pan with a long-handled spatula or wooden spoon. If the ingredients in the wok begin to dry out, add a splash of water.

COOK'S TIP
The advantage of cooking with a wok is that its gently sloping sides allow the heat to spread rapidly and evenly over the surface, allowing food to cook quickly, retaining flavor, color and nutrients.

Pork Saté with Crisp Noodle Cake

Crisp noodles are a popular and tasty accompaniment to saté, and are particularly good with the spicy saté sauce.

Serves 4–6

INGREDIENTS
1 pound lean pork
3 garlic cloves, finely chopped
1 tablespoon Thai curry powder
1 teaspoon ground cumin
1 teaspoon sugar
1 tablespoon fish sauce
6 tablespoons oil
12 ounces thin egg noodles
cilantro leaves, to garnish

FOR THE SATÉ SAUCE
2 tablespoons oil
2 garlic cloves, finely chopped
1 small onion, finely chopped
½ teaspoon hot chili powder
1 teaspoon Thai curry powder
1 cup coconut milk
1 tablespoon fish sauce
2 tablespoons sugar
juice of ½ lemon
½ cup plus 2 tablespoons crunchy
    peanut butter

pork · garlic · Thai curry powder · onion
ground cumin · sugar · fish sauce · thin egg noodles · cilantro
hot chili powder · coconut milk · lemon · crunchy peanut butter

1 Cut the pork into thin 2-inch-long strips. Mix the garlic, curry powder, cumin, sugar and fish sauce in a bowl. Stir in about 2 tablespoons of the oil. Add the meat to the bowl, toss to coat and let marinate in a cool place for at least 2 hours. Meanwhile, cook the noodles in a large saucepan of boiling water until just tender. Drain thoroughly.

2 Make the saté sauce. Heat the oil in a saucepan and sauté the garlic and onion with the chili powder and curry powder for 2–3 minutes. Stir in the coconut milk, fish sauce, sugar, lemon juice and peanut butter. Mix well. Reduce the heat and cook, stirring frequently, for about 20 minutes, or until the sauce thickens. Be careful not to let the sauce stick to the bottom of the pan or it will burn.

3 Heat about 1 tablespoon of the remaining oil in a frying pan. Spread the noodles evenly over the pan and fry for 4–5 minutes, until crisp and golden. Turn the noodle cake over carefully and cook the other side until crisp. Keep hot.

4 Drain the meat and thread it onto soaked, drained bamboo skewers. Cook under a hot broiler for 8–10 minutes, until cooked, turning occasionally and brushing with the remaining oil. Serve with wedges of noodle cake, accompanied by the saté sauce. Garnish with cilantro leaves.

Vegetable Spring Rolls with Sweet Chili Sauce

Vermicelli noodles need hardly any cooking before being stirred into the tasty vegetable filling.

Makes 20–24

INGREDIENTS
1 ounce rice vermicelli noodles
oil, for deep-frying
1 teaspoon grated fresh ginger root
2 scallions, finely shredded
2 ounces carrot, finely grated
2 ounces snow peas, thinly sliced
1 ounce young spinach leaves
¼ cup bean sprouts
1 tablespoon chopped fresh mint
1 tablespoon chopped cilantro
2 tablespoons fish sauce
20–24 spring roll wrappers,
    each 5 inches square
1 egg white, lightly beaten

FOR THE DIPPING SAUCE
¼ cup sugar
3½ tablespoons rice vinegar
2 red chiles, seeded and finely
    chopped

rice vermicelli noodles
scallions
snow peas
cilantro
bean sprouts
fish sauce
spring roll wrappers
red chiles

COOK'S TIP
Use peanut oil for this recipe or otherwise sunflower oil. Peanut oil has a distinct flavor and gives an authentic taste. Sunflower oil is milder but still very good.

1 First make the dipping sauce. Place the sugar and vinegar in a small pan with 2 tablespoons water. Heat gently, stirring until the sugar dissolves, then boil rapidly until it forms a light syrup. Stir in the chiles and let cool.

2 Soak the noodles according to the package instructions; rinse and drain well. Using scissors, snip the noodles into short lengths.

3 Heat 1 tablespoon of the oil in a wok and stir-fry the ginger and scallions for 15 seconds. Add the carrot and snow peas and stir-fry for 2–3 minutes. Add the spinach, bean sprouts, mint, cilantro, fish sauce and noodles and stir-fry for another minute. Set aside.

4 Take one spring roll wrapper and arrange it so that it faces you in a diamond shape. Place a spoonful of filling just below the center, then fold up the bottom point over the filling.

5 Fold in each side, then roll up tightly. Brush the end with beaten egg white and seal. Repeat this process until all the filling has been used.

6 Half-fill a wok with oil and heat to 350°F. Deep-fry the spring rolls in batches for 3–4 minutes, until golden. Drain. Serve hot with the chili sauce.

Japanese Chilled Noodles with Dashi Dip

This classic Japanese dish of cold noodles is known as *somen*. The noodles are surprisingly refreshing when eaten with fish or fried meats and the delicately flavored dip.

Serves 4–6

INGREDIENTS
1–2 tablespoons oil
2 medium eggs, beaten with a pinch of salt
1 sheet yaki-nori seaweed, finely shredded
½ bunch scallions, thinly sliced
wasabi paste, to taste
14 ounces dried somen noodles
ice cubes, for serving

FOR THE DIP
4 cups kombu and bonito stock or instant dashi
scant 1 cup Japanese soy sauce
1 tablespoon mirin

eggs

scallions

wasabi paste

mirin

kombu and bonito stock

soy sauce

dried somen noodles

1 Prepare the dashi dip in advance so that it has time to cool and chill. Using either kombu and bonito stock or instant dashi, bring all the ingredients to a boil. Let cool and chill thoroughly.

Meanwhile, heat a little oil in a frying pan. Pour in half the beaten eggs, tilting the pan to coat the bottom evenly. Let set, then turn the omelet over and cook the second side briefly. Turn out onto a board. Cook the remaining egg in the same way.

2 Let the omelets cool and then shred them finely. Place the shredded omelet, yaki-nori, scallions and wasabi in four small bowls.

3 Boil the somen noodles according to the package instructions and drain. Rinse the noodles thoroughly under cold running water, stirring with chopsticks, then drain thoroughly again.

4 Place the noodles on a large plate and set some ice cubes on top to keep them cool. Pour the cold dip into four small bowls. Noodles and accompaniments are dipped into the chilled dip before they are eaten.

Chinese-style Cabbage and Noodle Parcels

The noodles and Chinese mushrooms give a delightful Asian flavor to these traditional cabbage rolls. Serve with rice for a tasty meal.

Serves 4–6

INGREDIENTS
4 dried Chinese mushrooms, soaked
   in hot water until soft
2 ounces cellophane noodles,
   soaked in hot water until soft
1 pound ground pork
8 scallions, 2 finely chopped
2 garlic cloves, finely chopped
2 tablespoons fish sauce
12 large outer green cabbage leaves
salt and freshly ground black pepper

FOR THE SAUCE
2 tablespoons oil
1 small onion, finely chopped
2 garlic cloves, crushed
14-ounce can chopped plum
   tomatoes
pinch of sugar

Chinese mushrooms

scallions

cellophane noodles

ground pork

garlic

fish sauce

onion

chopped plum tomatoes

1 Drain the mushrooms, remove and discard the stems and coarsely chop the caps. Put them in a bowl. Next, drain the noodles and cut them into short lengths. Add the noodles to the bowl with the pork, chopped scallions and garlic. Season with the fish sauce and pepper.

2 Blanch the cabbage leaves a few at a time in a saucepan of salted boiling water for about 1 minute. Remove the leaves from the pan and refresh under cold water. Drain and dry on paper towels. Blanch the remaining scallions in the same fashion. Drain well. Fill one of the cabbage leaves with a generous spoonful of the pork and noodle filling. Taking hold of the corner closest to you, roll up the leaf sufficiently to enclose the filling, then tuck in the sides and continue rolling the leaf to make a tight parcel. Make more parcels in the same way.

5 Season the tomato mixture with salt, pepper and a pinch of sugar, then bring to the simmering point. Add the cabbage parcels. Cover and cook gently for 20–25 minutes, or until the filling is cooked. Taste the sauce to check the seasoning and serve at once.

3 Split each scallion lengthwise by cutting through the bulb and then tearing upward. Tie each of the cabbage parcels with a length of scallion.

4 To make the sauce, heat the oil in a large frying pan and add the onion and garlic. Sauté for 2 minutes, until soft. Pour the plum tomatoes into a bowl. Mash with a fork, then add to the onion mixture.

COOK'S TIP
If at any time the tomato sauce looks a little dry, add some water or vegetable stock to the pan and stir thoroughly.

Thai Pork Spring Rolls

Crunchy spring rolls are as popular in Thai cuisine as they are in Chinese. In this version they are filled with noodles, garlic and pork.

Makes about 24

INGREDIENTS

4–6 dried Chinese mushrooms, soaked in hot water until soft
2 ounces cellophane noodles
2 tablespoons oil
2 garlic cloves, chopped
2 red chiles, seeded and chopped
8 ounces ground pork
2 ounces cooked peeled shrimp, chopped
2 tablespoons fish sauce
1 teaspoon sugar
freshly ground black pepper
1 carrot, very finely sliced
2 ounces bamboo shoots, chopped
¼ cup bean sprouts
2 scallions, chopped
1 tablespoon chopped cilantro
2 tablespoons all-purpose flour
24 x 6-inch square spring roll wrappers
oil, for deep-frying
Thai sweet chili sauce, to serve (optional)

Chinese mushrooms

cellophane noodles

garlic

ground pork

cooked shrimp

fish sauce

bean sprouts

cilantro

spring roll wrappers

1 Drain and finely chop the Chinese mushrooms. Remove and discard the stems. Soak the noodles in hot water until soft, then drain. Cut into short lengths, about 2 inches.

2 Heat the oil in a wok or large frying pan, add the garlic and chiles and fry for 30 seconds. Add the pork and stir-fry for a few minutes, until the meat is browned. Add the noodles, mushrooms and shrimp. Season with fish sauce, sugar and pepper. Pour into a bowl. Add the carrot, bamboo shoots, bean sprouts, scallions and cilantro and stir well to mix.

3 Put the flour in a small bowl and blend with a little water to make a paste. Place a spoonful of filling in the center of a spring roll wrapper.

4 Turn the bottom edge over to cover the filling, then fold in the left and right sides. Roll the wrapper up almost to the top edge. Brush the top edge with flour paste and seal. Repeat with the rest of the wrappers.

5 Heat the oil in a wok or deep-fat fryer. Slide in the spring rolls a few at a time and fry until crisp and golden brown. Remove with a slotted spoon and drain on paper towels. Serve with Thai sweet chili sauce to dip them into, if you like.

Fried Monkfish Coated with Rice Noodles

These marinated medallions of fish are coated in rice vermicelli and deep-fried—they taste as good as they look.

Serves 4

INGREDIENTS
1 pound monkfish
1 teaspoon grated fresh ginger root
1 garlic clove, finely chopped
2 tablespoons light soy sauce
6 ounces rice vermicelli noodles
2 ounces cornstarch
2 eggs, beaten
oil, for deep-frying
banana leaves, to serve (optional)

FOR THE DIPPING SAUCE
2 tablespoons light soy sauce
2 tablespoons rice vinegar
1 tablespoon sugar
salt and freshly ground black pepper
2 red chiles, seeded and thinly sliced
1 scallion, thinly sliced

monkfish
fresh ginger root
garlic
light soy sauce
rice vermicelli noodles
eggs
rice vinegar
sugar
red chiles
scallions

1 Cut the monkfish into 1-inch-thick medallions. Place in a dish and add the ginger, garlic and soy sauce. Let marinate for 10 minutes. For the dipping sauce, heat the soy sauce, vinegar and sugar in a saucepan until boiling. Add the salt and pepper. Remove from the heat and add the chiles and scallion.

2 Using kitchen scissors, cut the noodles into 1½-inch lengths. Spread them out in a shallow bowl.

3 Coat the fish medallions in cornstarch, dip in beaten egg and cover with noodles, pressing them onto the fish so that they stick.

4 Deep-fry the coated fish in hot oil, 2 or 3 pieces at a time, until the noodle coating is crisp and golden brown. Drain and serve hot on banana leaves if you like, accompanied by the dipping sauce.

Deep-fried Wonton Cushions with Sambal Kecap

These delicious, golden packages, called *pansit goreng*, are popular in Indonesia as party fare or for a quick snack.

Makes 40

INGREDIENTS
4 ounces pork fillet, trimmed and
    sliced
8 ounces cooked peeled shrimp
2–3 garlic cloves, crushed
2 scallions, roughly chopped
1 tablespoon cornstarch
about 40 wonton wrappers
oil, for deep-frying
salt and freshly ground black pepper

FOR THE SAMBAL KECAP
1–2 red chiles, seeded and sliced
1–2 garlic cloves, crushed
3 tablespoons dark soy sauce
3–4 tablespoons lemon or
    lime juice

1 Grind the slices of pork finely in a food processor. Add the shrimp, garlic, scallions and cornstarch. Season and then process briefly.

2 Place a little of the prepared filling onto each wonton wrapper, just off center, with the wrapper positioned like a diamond in front of you. Dampen all the edges, except for the uppermost corner of the diamond.

cornstarch

pork fillet

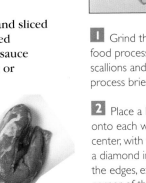
cooked shrimp

garlic

scallions

wonton wrappers

red chiles

lemon juice

dark soy sauce

3 Lift the corner nearest you toward the filling and then roll up the wrapper to cover the filling. Turn over. Bring the two extreme corners together, sealing one on top of the other. Squeeze lightly to plump up the filling. Repeat the process until all the wrappers and the filling are used up. The prepared "cushions" and any leftover wonton wrappers can be frozen at this stage.

4 Meanwhile, prepare the sambal. Mix the chiles and garlic together and then stir in the dark soy sauce, lemon or lime juice and 1–2 tablespoons water. Pour into a serving bowl and set aside.

5 Deep-fry the wonton cushions in hot oil, a few at a time, for 2–3 minutes, or until cooked through, crisp and golden brown. Serve on a large platter together with the sambal kecap.

Alfalfa Crab Salad with Crisp Fried Noodles

The crisp noodles make a delicious contrast, both in flavor and texture, with this healthy mixture of crab and vegetables.

Serves 4–6

INGREDIENTS

oil, for deep-frying
2 ounces Chinese rice noodles
5 ounces frozen lump crabmeat, thawed
½ cup alfalfa sprouts
1 small head iceberg lettuce
4 sprigs cilantro, roughly chopped
1 ripe tomato, peeled, seeded and diced
4 sprigs fresh mint, roughly chopped, plus an extra sprig to garnish

FOR THE SESAME LIME DRESSING

3 tablespoons vegetable oil
1 teaspoon sesame oil
½ small red chile, seeded and finely chopped
1 piece preserved ginger in syrup, cut into matchsticks
2 teaspoons ginger syrup
2 teaspoons light soy sauce
juice of ½ lime

Chinese rice noodles

crabmeat

alfalfa sprouts

iceberg lettuce

tomato

mint

cilantro

red chile

lime

1 First make the dressing. Combine the vegetable and sesame oils in a bowl. Add the chile, ginger, ginger syrup and soy sauce and stir in the lime juice. Set aside.

2 Heat the oil in a wok or deep-fat fryer to 385°F. Fry the noodles, one handful at a time, until crisp. Lift out and drain on paper towels.

3 Flake the crabmeat into a bowl and toss with the alfalfa sprouts.

4 Finely chop the lettuce and mix with the cilantro, tomato and mint. Place in a bowl, top with the noodles and the crabmeat and alfalfa salad and garnish with a sprig of mint. Serve with the sesame lime dressing.

Smoked Trout and Noodle Salad

This salad is a wonderful example of how well noodles can combine with Mediterranean ingredients, such as trout, capers and tomatoes.

Serves 4

INGREDIENTS
8 ounces somen noodles
2 smoked trout, skinned and boned
2 hard-boiled eggs, coarsely
   chopped
2 tablespoons snipped chives
lime halves, to serve (optional)

FOR THE DRESSING
6 ripe plum tomatoes
2 shallots, finely chopped
2 tablespoons tiny capers, rinsed
2 tablespoons chopped fresh
   tarragon
finely grated zest and juice of
   ½ orange
4 tablespoons extra-virgin olive oil
salt and freshly ground black pepper

somen noodles   *smoked trout*

chives

hard-boiled eggs   *olive oil*   *orange*

plum tomatoes   *shallots*

fresh tarragon

1 To make the dressing, cut the tomatoes in half, remove the cores and cut the flesh into chunks. Place in a bowl with the shallots, capers, tarragon, orange zest and juice and olive oil. Season with salt and pepper and mix well. Let the dressing marinate for 1–2 hours.

2 Cook the noodles in a large saucepan of boiling water until just tender. Drain and rinse under cold running water. Drain well.

COOK'S TIP
Choose tomatoes that are firm, bright in color and have a smooth surface, avoiding any with blotched or cracked skins.

3 Toss the noodles with the dressing, then adjust the seasoning to taste. Arrange the noodles on a large serving platter or individual plates.

4 Flake the smoked trout over the noodles, then sprinkle the coarsely chopped eggs and snipped chives over the top. Serve the lime halves on the side, if you like.

Beef Noodle Soup

This rich, satisfying soup is packed with all sorts of flavors and textures, brought together with delicious egg noodles.

Serves 4

INGREDIENTS

¼ ounce dried porcini mushrooms
6 scallions
4 ounces carrots
12 ounces sirloin steak
about 2 tablespoons oil
1 garlic clove, crushed
1-inch piece fresh ginger root,
    finely chopped
5 cups beef stock
3 tablespoons light soy sauce
4 tablespoons dry sherry
3 ounces thin egg noodles
3 ounces spinach, shredded
salt and freshly ground black pepper

dried porcini mushrooms *scallions*

carrots *rump steak*

garlic

fresh ginger root *dry sherry*

beef stock

light soy sauce

egg noodles *spinach*

1 Break the mushrooms into small pieces, place in a bowl, pour ⅔ cup boiling water over and let soak for 15 minutes. Strain the mushrooms, squeezing as much liquid from them as possible. Reserve the liquid.

2 Meanwhile, cut the scallions and carrots into 2-inch-long strips. Trim any fat from the meat and slice into thin strips.

3 Heat the oil in a large saucepan and cook the beef in batches until browned, adding a little more oil if necessary. Remove the beef with a slotted spoon and drain on paper towels.

4 Add the garlic, ginger, scallions and carrots to the pan and stir-fry for 3 minutes.

5 Add the beef stock, the mushrooms and their soaking liquid, the soy sauce, sherry and plenty of seasoning. Bring to a boil and simmer, covered, for 10 minutes.

6 Break up the noodles slightly and add to the pan, with the spinach. Simmer gently for 5 minutes, or until the beef is tender. Adjust the seasoning before serving.

Chiang Mai Noodle Soup

This richly flavored and aromatic noodle soup is a signature dish of the Thai city of Chiang Mai.

Serves 4–6

INGREDIENTS
2½ cups coconut milk
2 tablespoons red curry paste
1 teaspoon ground turmeric
1 pound chicken thighs, boned and
    cut into bite-size chunks
2½ cups chicken stock
¼ cup fish sauce
1 tablespoon dark soy sauce
juice of ½–1 lime
1 pound fresh egg noodles,
    blanched briefly in boiling water
salt and freshly ground black pepper

FOR THE GARNISH
3 scallions, chopped
4 red chiles
4 shallots, chopped
¼ cup sliced pickled mustard
    greens, rinsed
2 tablespoons fried sliced garlic
cilantro sprigs

coconut
milk

red curry
paste

ground
tumeric

chicken thighs

chicken
stock

fish
sauce

dark soy
sauce

lime

fresh egg
noodles

red
chiles

scallions

cilantro

 Pour about one-third of the coconut milk into a saucepan and bring to a boil, stirring frequently until it separates.

 Add the curry paste and ground turmeric, stir to mix completely and cook for a few minutes, until blended.

 Add the chicken pieces to the saucepan and stir-fry for about 2 minutes. Make sure that all the chunks of meat are coated with the paste.

 Add the remaining coconut milk, stock, fish sauce, soy sauce and seasoning. Simmer for 7–10 minutes. Remove from the heat and add the lime juice.

Reheat the noodles in boiling water, then drain. Divide the noodles and chicken among the bowls and ladle the hot soup over. Top with the garnishes.

Pork and Pickled Mustard Greens Soup

The pickled mustard greens (also called pickled cabbage) give the flavor while the cellophane noodles bring texture to this traditional Thai soup.

Serves 4–6

INGREDIENTS

8 ounces pickled mustard greens, soaked
2 ounces cellophane noodles, soaked
1 tablespoon oil
4 garlic cloves, finely sliced
4 cups chicken stock
1 pound pork ribs, cut into large chunks
2 tablespoons fish sauce
pinch of sugar
freshly ground black pepper
2 red chiles, seeded and finely sliced, to garnish

cellophane noodles

garlic *chicken stock*

fish sauce

pork ribs

red chiles

1 Drain the pickled mustard greens and cut them into bite-size pieces. Taste to check that the seasoning is to your liking. If they are too salty, soak them in water for a little bit longer.

2 Drain the cellophane noodles and cut them into short lengths.

3 Heat the oil in a small frying pan, add the garlic and stir-fry until golden, taking care not to let it burn. Transfer the mixture to a bowl and set aside.

4 Put the stock in a saucepan, bring to a boil, then add the pork and simmer gently for 10–15 minutes. Add the pickled mustard greens and cellophane noodles. Bring back to a boil. Season to taste with fish sauce, sugar and freshly ground black pepper. Serve hot, topped with the fried garlic and red chiles.

Hanoi Beef and Noodle Soup

Millions of North Vietnamese eat this fragrant noodle soup every day for breakfast.

Serves 4–6

INGREDIENTS

1 onion
3–3½ pounds stewing beef
1-inch piece fresh ginger root, peeled
1 star anise
1 bay leaf
2 whole cloves
½ teaspoon fennel seeds
1 piece cassia or cinnamon stick
fish sauce, to taste
juice of 1 lime
5 ounces beef tenderloin
1 pound fresh flat rice noodles
salt and freshly ground black pepper
handful of cilantro leaves and lime
    wedges, to garnish

FOR THE ACCOMPANIMENTS

1 small red onion, sliced into rings
½ cup bean sprouts
2 red chiles, seeded and sliced
2 scallions, finely sliced

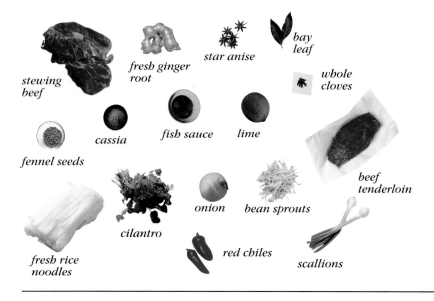

stewing beef · fresh ginger root · star anise · bay leaf · whole cloves · cassia · fish sauce · lime · beef tenderloin · fennel seeds · cilantro · onion · bean sprouts · fresh rice noodles · red chiles · scallions

1 Cut the onion in half. Broil under high heat, cut side up, until the exposed sides are caramelized and deep brown.

3 Add 12½ cups water, bring to a boil, reduce the heat and simmer gently for 2–3 hours, skimming off the fat and scum from time to time.

2 Cut the stewing beef into large chunks and then place in a large saucepan or stockpot. Add the caramelized onion with the ginger, star anise, bay leaf, cloves, fennel seeds and cassia or cinnamon stick.

4 Using a slotted spoon, remove the meat from the stock; when cool enough to handle, cut into small pieces. Strain the stock and return to the pan or stockpot together with the meat. Bring back to a boil and season with the fish sauce, lime juice and salt and pepper to taste.

5 Slice the tenderloin very thinly and then chill until required. Cook the noodles in a large pan of boiling water until just tender. Drain and divide among individual serving bowls. Arrange the thinly sliced tenderloin over the noodles, pour the hot stock on top and garnish with cilantro and lime wedges. Serve, offering the accompaniments in separate bowls.

Malaysian Spicy Shrimp and Noodle Soup

This is a Malaysian version of Hanoi Beef and Noodle Soup using fish and shrimp instead of beef. If laksa noodles aren't available, flat rice noodles can be used instead.

Serves 4–6

INGREDIENTS
1 ounce unsalted cashew nuts
3 shallots, or 1 medium onion, sliced
2-inch piece lemongrass, shredded
2 cloves garlic, crushed
2 tablespoons oil
1 tablespoon shrimp paste or 1 tablespoon fish sauce
1 tablespoon mild curry paste
1⅔ cups coconut milk
½ chicken bouillon cube
3 curry leaves (optional)
1 pound white fish fillets, e.g. cod, haddock or whiting
8 ounces shrimp, fresh or cooked
5 ounces laksa noodles, soaked for 10 minutes before cooking
1 small head romaine lettuce, shredded
½ cup bean sprouts
3 scallions, cut into lengths
½ cucumber, thinly sliced
shrimp crackers, to serve

1 Grind the cashew nuts using a mortar and pestle and then spoon into a food processor and process with the shallots or onion, lemongrass and garlic.

2 Heat the oil in a large wok or saucepan, add the cashew and onion mixture and fry for 1–2 minutes, until the mixture begins to brown.

3 Add the shrimp paste or fish sauce and curry paste, followed by the coconut milk, bouillon cube and curry leaves, if using. Simmer for 10 minutes.

cashew nuts (unsalted)

garlic *shrimp paste*

curry paste

coconut milk *curry leaves* *white fish fillets* *shrimp*

lemongrass *bean sprouts* *scallions* *cucumber* *laksa noodles*

shallots

4 Cut the fish into bite-size pieces. Add the fish and shrimp to the coconut stock, immersing them with a frying basket or a slotted spoon. Cook for 3–4 minutes, until the fish is tender. Cook the noodles according to the instructions on the package.

Mock Shark's Fin Soup

Shark's fin soup is a renowned delicacy. In this vegetarian version, cellophane noodles mimic shark's fin needles.

Serves 4–6

INGREDIENTS

4 dried Chinese mushrooms
1½ tablespoons dried wood ears
4 ounces cellophane noodles
2 tablespoons oil
2 carrots, cut into fine strips
4 ounces canned bamboo shoots, rinsed, drained and cut into fine strips
4 cups vegetable stock
1 tablespoon light soy sauce
1 tablespoon arrowroot or potato flour
1 egg white, beaten (optional)
1 teaspoon sesame oil
salt and freshly ground black pepper
2 scallions, finely chopped, to garnish
Chinese red vinegar, to serve (optional)

dried Chinese mushrooms

dried wood ears

cellophane noodles

carrots

bamboo shoots

vegetable stock

light soy sauce

egg

sesame oil

scallions

1 Soak the mushrooms and wood ears separately in warm water for 20 minutes. Drain. Remove the mushroom stems and slice the caps thinly. Cut the wood ears into fine strips, discarding any hard bits. Soak the noodles in hot water until soft. Drain and cut into short lengths.

2 Heat the oil in a large saucepan. Add the mushrooms and stir-fry for 2 minutes. Add the wood ears, stir-fry for 2 minutes, then stir in the carrots, bamboo shoots and noodles.

3 Add the stock to the pan. Bring to a boil, then simmer for 15–20 minutes.

4 Season with salt, pepper and soy sauce. Blend the arrowroot or potato flour with about 2 tablespoons water. Pour into the soup, stirring all the time to prevent lumps from forming as the soup continues to simmer.

5 Remove the pan from the heat. Stir in the egg white, if using, so that it sets to form small threads in the hot soup. Stir in the sesame oil, then pour the soup into individual bowls. Sprinkle each portion with chopped scallions and offer the Chinese red vinegar separately, if using.

Noodles, Chicken and Shrimp in Coconut Broth

This dish takes a well-flavored broth and adds noodles and a delicious combination of other ingredients to make a satisfying main course.

Serves 8

INGREDIENTS
2 onions, quartered
1-inch piece fresh ginger root, sliced
2 garlic cloves
4 macadamia nuts or 8 almonds
1–2 chiles, seeded and sliced
2 lemongrass stems, lower
    2 inches sliced
2-inch fresh turmeric, peeled and
    sliced, or 1 teaspoon ground
    turmeric
1 tablespoon coriander seeds,
    dry-fried
1 teaspoon cumin seeds, dry-fried
4 tablespoons oil
1⅔ cups coconut milk
6¼ cups chicken stock
13 ounces rice noodles, soaked in
    cold water
12 ounces cooked tiger shrimp
salt and freshly ground black pepper

FOR THE GARNISH
4 hard-boiled eggs, quartered
8 ounces cooked chicken, chopped
1 cup bean sprouts
1 bunch scallions, shredded
deep-fried onions (optional)

1 Place the quartered onions, ginger, garlic and nuts in a food processor with the chiles, sliced lemongrass and turmeric. Process to a paste. Alternatively, pound all the ingredients with a mortar and pestle. Grind the coriander and cumin seeds coarsely and add to the paste.

2 Heat the oil in a pan and fry the spice paste, without coloring, to bring out the flavors. Add the coconut milk, stock and seasoning and simmer for 5–10 minutes.

3 Meanwhile, drain the rice noodles and plunge them into a large pan of salted boiling water for 2 minutes. Remove from the heat and drain well. Rinse thoroughly with plenty of cold water, to halt the cooking process.

4 Add the shrimp to the soup just before serving and heat through for a minute or two. Arrange the garnishes in separate bowls. All guests help themselves to noodles, add soup, eggs, chicken and bean sprouts and then scatter shredded scallions and deep-fried onions on top.

COOK'S TIP

To dry-fry spices, heat a small, heavy pan over medium heat for 1 minute, add the spices and cook for 2–3 minutes, stirring frequently. Remove from the heat and grind the spices using a mortar and pestle.

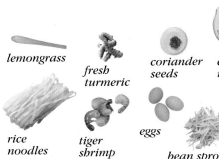

lemongrass

fresh turmeric

coriander seeds

coconut milk

chicken

rice noodles

tiger shrimp

eggs

bean sprouts

scallions

Beef Soup with Noodles and Meatballs

Egg noodles and spicy meatballs make this a really sustaining main soup-dish. In Asia, it is often served from street stalls.

Serves 6

INGREDIENTS

1 pound dried medium egg noodles
3 tablespoons sunflower oil
1 large onion, finely sliced
2 garlic cloves, crushed
1-inch piece fresh ginger root, cut
    into thin matchsticks
5 cups beef stock
2 tablespoons dark soy sauce
2 celery stalks, finely sliced, leaves
    reserved
6 bok choy leaves, cut into bite-size
    pieces
1 handful snow peas, cut
    into strips
salt and freshly ground black pepper

FOR THE MEATBALLS

1 large onion, roughly chopped
1–2 red chiles, seeded and chopped
2 garlic cloves, crushed
1 tablespoon shrimp paste
1 pound lean ground beef
1 tablespoon ground coriander
1 teaspoon ground cumin
2 teaspoons dark soy sauce
1 teaspoon dark brown sugar
juice of ½ lemon
a little beaten egg

red chiles

garlic

ground beef

ground coriander

ground cumin

onion

bok choy

dark soy sauce

dark brown sugar

lemon juice

snow peas

fresh ginger root

beef stock

egg

celery

dried egg noodles

COOK'S TIP

Shrimp paste, or *terasi*, has a strong, salty, distinctive flavor and smell. Use sparingly if unsure of its flavor.

1 For the meatballs, put the onion, chiles, garlic and shrimp paste in a food processor. Process in short bursts, taking care not to overchop the onion.

2 Put the meat in a large bowl. Stir in the onion mixture. Add the ground coriander and cumin, soy sauce, brown sugar, lemon juice and seasoning.

3 Bind the mixture with a little beaten egg and shape into small balls.

4 Cook the noodles in a large pan of boiling salted water for 3–4 minutes, or until al dente. Drain in a colander and rinse with plenty of cold water. Set aside. Heat the oil in a wide pan and sauté the onion, garlic and ginger until soft but not browned. Add the stock and soy sauce and bring to a boil.

5 Add the meatballs, half-cover and simmer until they are cooked, 5–8 minutes. Just before serving, add the sliced celery and, after 2 minutes, the bok choy and snow peas. Adjust the seasoning. Divide the noodles among soup bowls, pour the soup on top and garnish with the reserved celery leaves.

Japanese Noodle Casseroles

Traditionally, these individual casseroles are cooked in earthenware pots. *Nabe* means "pot" and *yaki* means "to heat," providing the Japanese name *nabeyaki udon* for this dish.

Serves 4

INGREDIENTS
4 ounces boneless chicken thighs
½ teaspoon salt
½ teaspoon sake or dry white wine
½ teaspoon light soy sauce
1 leek, washed thoroughly
4 ounces fresh spinach, trimmed
11 ounces dried udon noodles or
    1¼ pounds fresh udon noodles
4 shiitake mushrooms, stems
    removed
4 medium eggs
shichimi, or seven-flavor spice, to
    serve (optional)

FOR THE SOUP
6 cups kombu and bonito stock or
    instant dashi
1½ tablespoons light soy sauce
1 teaspoon salt
1 tablespoon mirin

light soy sauce *leeks*

chicken thighs

sake

spinach

shiitake mushrooms

udon noodles

eggs *kombu and bonito stock* *mirin*

1 Cut the chicken into small chunks and sprinkle with the salt, sake or wine and soy sauce. Cut the leek diagonally into 1½-inch slices.

3 For the soup, bring the kombu and bonito stock, soy sauce, salt and mirin to a boil in a saucepan and add the chicken and leek. Skim the broth, then simmer for 5 minutes.

2 Boil the spinach for 1–2 minutes, then drain and soak in cold water for 1 minute. Drain, squeeze lightly, then cut into 1½-inch lengths. If using dried udon noodles, boil them according to the package instructions, allowing 3 minutes less than the stated cooking time. Place fresh udon noodles in boiling water, disentangle, then drain.

4 Divide the udon noodles among four individual flameproof casseroles. Pour the soup, chicken and leeks into the casseroles. Place over medium heat and add the shiitake mushrooms. Gently break an egg into each casserole. Cover and simmer gently for 2 minutes.

5 Divide the spinach among the casseroles and simmer, covered, for another minute.

6 Serve immediately, standing the hot casseroles on plates or table mats. Sprinkle seven-flavor spice over the casseroles if you like.

COOK'S TIP

Assorted tempura using vegetables such as sweet potato, carrot and shiitake mushrooms, and fish such as squid and shrimp, could be served in these casseroles instead of chicken and egg.

Crisp Noodles with Mixed Vegetables

In this dish, rice vermicelli noodles are deep-fried until crisp, then tossed into a colorful selection of stir-fried vegetables.

Serves 3–4

INGREDIENTS
2 large carrots
2 zucchini
4 scallions
4 ounces yard-long beans or green beans
4 ounces dried rice vermicelli or cellophane noodles
oil, for deep-frying
1-inch piece fresh ginger root, cut into shreds
1 red chile, seeded and sliced
4 ounces fresh shiitake or button mushrooms, thickly sliced
a few Chinese cabbage leaves, coarsely shredded
⅓ cup bean sprouts
2 tablespoons light soy sauce
2 tablespoons Chinese rice wine
1 teaspoon sugar
2 tablespoons roughly torn cilantro leaves

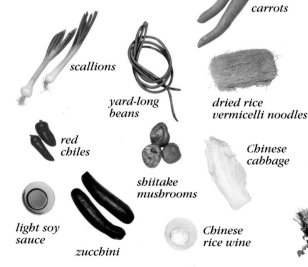

scallions

carrots

yard-long beans

dried rice vermicelli noodles

fresh ginger root

red chiles

shiitake mushrooms

Chinese cabbage

bean sprouts

light soy sauce

zucchini

Chinese rice wine

cilantro

COOK'S TIP
If a milder flavor is preferred, remove the seeds from the chile.

1 Cut the carrots and zucchini into fine sticks. Shred the scallions into similar-size pieces. Trim the beans. If using yard-long beans, cut them into short lengths.

2 Break the noodles into lengths of about 3 inches. Half-fill a wok with oil and heat it to 350°F. Deep-fry the raw noodles, a handful at a time, for 1–2 minutes, until puffed and crisp. Drain on paper towels. Carefully pour off all but 2 tablespoons of the oil.

3 Reheat the oil in the wok. When hot, add the beans and stir-fry for 2–3 minutes. Add the ginger, red chile, mushrooms, carrots and zucchini and stir-fry for 1–2 minutes.

4 Add the cabbage, bean sprouts and scallions. Stir-fry for 1 minute, then add the soy sauce, rice wine and sugar. Cook, stirring, for about 30 seconds.

5 Add the noodles and cilantro and toss to mix, taking care not to crush the noodles too much. Serve at once, piled on a plate.

Chinese Mushrooms with Cellophane Noodles

Red fermented bean curd adds extra flavor to this hearty vegetarian dish. It is brick red in color, with a very strong, cheesy flavor.

Serves 3–4

INGREDIENTS
4 ounces dried Chinese mushrooms
1 ounce dried wood ears
4 ounces dried bean curd
2 tablespoons oil
2 garlic cloves, finely chopped
2 slices fresh ginger root, finely chopped
10 Szechuan peppercorns, crushed
1 tablespoon red fermented bean curd
½ star anise
pinch of sugar
1–2 tablespoons dark soy sauce
2 ounces cellophane noodles, soaked in hot water until soft
salt

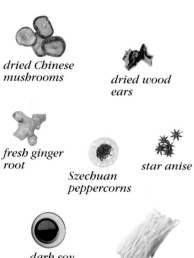

dried Chinese mushrooms

dried wood ears

fresh ginger root

Szechuan peppercorns

star anise

dark soy sauce

cellophane noodles

1 Soak the Chinese mushrooms and wood ears separately in bowls of hot water for 30 minutes. Break the dried bean curd into pieces and soak in water according to the package instructions.

2 Strain the mushrooms, squeezing as much liquid from them as possible. Strain and reserve the liquid. Discard the stems and cut the caps in half if large. Drain the wood ears, rinse and drain again. Cut off any gritty parts, then cut each wood ear into two or three pieces.

3 Heat the oil in a heavy pan and sauté the garlic, ginger and Szechuan peppercorns for a few seconds. Add the mushrooms and red fermented bean curd, mix lightly and cook for 5 minutes.

4 Add the reserved mushroom liquid to the pan, with sufficient water to completely cover the mushrooms. Add the star anise, sugar and soy sauce, then cover and simmer for 30 seconds. Add the chopped wood ears and reconstituted bean curd pieces to the pan. Cover and cook for about 10 minutes.

5 Drain the cellophane noodles, add them to the mixture and cook for another 10 minutes, until tender, adding more liquid if necessary. Add salt to taste and serve.

Stir-fried Bean Curd with Noodles

This is a satisfying dish that is both tasty and easy to make.

Serves 4

INGREDIENTS

8 ounces firm bean curd
peanut oil, for deep-frying
6 ounces medium egg noodles
1 tablespoon sesame oil
1 teaspoon cornstarch
2 teaspoons dark soy sauce
2 tablespoons Chinese rice wine
1 teaspoon sugar
6–8 scallions, cut diagonally into
    1-inch lengths
3 garlic cloves, sliced
1 green chile, seeded and sliced
4 ounces Chinese cabbage leaves,
    coarsely shredded (about 2 cups)
¼ cup bean sprouts
½ cup cashew nuts, toasted

bean curd

egg noodles

sesame oil

dark soy sauce

garlic

Chinese cabbage

scallions

green chile

bean sprouts

cashew nuts

1 If in water, drain the bean curd and pat dry with paper towels. Cut it into 1-inch cubes. Half-fill a wok with peanut oil and heat to 350°F. Deep-fry the bean curd in batches for 1–2 minutes, until golden and crisp. Drain on paper towels. Carefully pour all but 2 tablespoons of the oil from the wok.

2 Cook the noodles. Rinse them thoroughly under cold water and drain well. Toss in 2 teaspoons of the sesame oil and set aside. In a bowl, blend together the cornstarch, soy sauce, rice wine, sugar and remaining sesame oil.

3 Reheat the 2 tablespoons of peanut oil and, when hot, add the scallions, garlic, chile, cabbage and bean sprouts. Stir-fry for 1–2 minutes.

4 Add the bean curd, noodles and cornstarch mixture. Cook, stirring, for about 1 minute, until well mixed. Sprinkle the cashew nuts over. Serve at once.

Egg Noodle Stir-fry

The thick egg noodles and potatoes, along with the vegetables, make this a satisfying and healthy main dish. If possible, use fresh egg noodles, which are available at most large supermarkets.

Serves 4

INGREDIENTS
2 eggs
1 teaspoon chili powder
1 teaspoon ground turmeric
¼ cup oil
1 large onion, finely sliced
2 red chiles, seeded and finely sliced
1 tablespoon light soy sauce
2 large cooked potatoes, cut into
    small cubes
6 pieces fried bean curd, sliced
1 cup bean sprouts
4 ounces green beans, blanched
12 ounces fresh thick egg noodles
salt and freshly ground black pepper
sliced scallions, to garnish

eggs

chile powder

ground turmeric

onion

red chiles

light soy sauce

potatoes

fried bean curd

bean sprouts

green beans

fresh thick egg noodles

scallions

COOK'S TIP
Ideally, wear gloves when preparing chiles; if you don't, certainly wash your hands thoroughly afterward. Keep your hands away from your eyes, as chiles will sting them.

1 Beat the eggs lightly, then strain them into a bowl. Heat a lightly greased omelet pan. Pour in half of the beaten egg just to cover the bottom of the pan. When the egg is set, carefully turn the omelet over and briefly cook the other side.

2 Slide the omelet onto a plate, blot with paper towels, roll up and cut into narrow strips. Make a second omelet in the same way and slice. Set the omelet strips aside for the garnish.

3 In a cup, mix together the chili powder and turmeric. Form a paste by stirring in a little water. Heat the oil in a wok or large frying pan. Sauté the onion until soft. Reduce the heat and add the chile paste, sliced chiles and soy sauce. Cook for 2–3 minutes.

4 Add the potatoes and cook for about 2 minutes, mixing well with the chiles. Add the bean curd, then the bean sprouts, green beans and noodles.

5 Gently stir-fry until the noodles are evenly coated and heated through. Take care not to break up the potatoes or the bean curd. Season with salt and pepper. Serve hot, garnished with the omelet strips and scallion slices.

Peanut and Vegetable Noodles

Add any of your favorite vegetables to this recipe, which is quick to make for a great midweek supper.

Serves 3–4

INGREDIENTS

8 ounces medium egg noodles
2 tablespoons olive oil
2 garlic cloves, crushed
1 large onion, roughly chopped
1 red bell pepper, seeded and
    roughly chopped
1 yellow bell pepper, seeded and
    roughly chopped
12 ounces zucchini, roughly
    chopped
generous ½ cup roasted unsalted
    peanuts, roughly chopped

FOR THE DRESSING

¼ cup olive oil
grated zest and juice of 1 lemon
1 red chile, seeded and finely
    chopped
3 tablespoons chopped fresh chives,
    plus extra to garnish
1–2 tablespoons balsamic vinegar
salt and white pepper

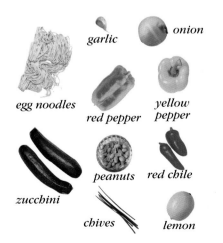

garlic onion

egg noodles
red pepper yellow pepper

zucchini peanuts red chile

chives lemon

1 Soak the noodles according to the package instructions and drain well.

2 Meanwhile, heat the oil in a very large frying pan or wok and cook the garlic and onion for 3–4 minutes, until beginning to soften. Add the peppers and zucchini and cook, over medium heat, for another 15 minutes, until beginning to soften and brown. Add the peanuts and cook for another minute.

3 Make the dressing. In a bowl, whisk together the olive oil, grated lemon zest and 3 tablespoons lemon juice, the chile, the chopped fresh chives, plenty of salt and pepper and balsamic vinegar to taste.

4 Toss the noodles into the vegetables and stir-fry to heat through. Add the dressing, stir to coat thoroughly and serve immediately, garnished with chopped fresh chives.

Five-spice Vegetable Noodles

Vary this vegetable stir-fry by substituting mushrooms, bamboo shoots, bean sprouts, snow peas or water chestnuts for some or all of the vegetables suggested below.

Serves 3–4

INGREDIENTS

8 ounces dried thin or medium egg
   noodles
2 tablespoons sesame oil
2 carrots
1 celery stalk
1 small fennel bulb
2 zucchini, halved and sliced
1 red chile, seeded and chopped
1-inch piece fresh ginger root, grated
1 garlic clove, crushed
1½ teaspoons Chinese five-spice
   powder
½ teaspoon ground cinnamon
4 scallions, sliced
sliced red chile, to garnish (optional)

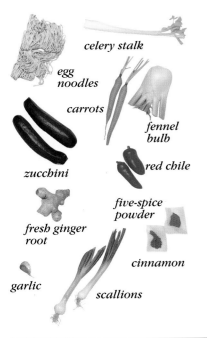

celery stalk

egg noodles

carrots

fennel bulb

zucchini

red chile

fresh ginger root

five-spice powder

cinnamon

garlic

scallions

1 Bring a large pan of salted water to a boil. Add the noodles and cook for 2–3 minutes, until just tender. Drain the noodles, return them to the pan and toss with a little of the sesame oil. Set aside.

2 Cut the carrot and celery into julienne strips. Cut the fennel bulb in half and cut away the hard core. Cut into slices, then cut the slices into thin strips.

3 Heat the remaining sesame oil in a wok until very hot. Add all the vegetables, including the chopped chile, and stir-fry for 7–8 minutes. Add the ginger and garlic and stir-fry for 2 minutes, then add the spices. Cook for 1 minute.

4 Add the scallions, stir-fry for 1 minute, then stir in ½ cup warm water and cook for 1 minute. Stir in the noodles and toss well together. Serve sprinkled with sliced red chile, if you like.

Noodles with Asparagus and Saffron Sauce

The asparagus, wine and cream give a distinctly French flavor to this elegant and delicious noodle dish.

Serves 4

INGREDIENTS
1 pound young asparagus
2 tablespoons butter
2 shallots, finely chopped
2 tablespoons white wine
1 cup heavy cream
pinch of saffron threads
grated zest and juice of ½ lemon
1 cup garden peas
12 ounces somen noodles
½ bunch chervil, roughly chopped
salt and freshly ground black pepper
grated Parmesan cheese (optional)

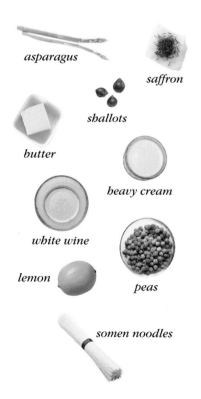

asparagus

saffron

shallots

butter

heavy cream

white wine

lemon

peas

somen noodles

1 Cut off the asparagus tips (about 2-inch lengths), then slice the remaining spears into short rounds. Soak the saffron in 2 tablespoons boiling water for a few minutes, until softened.

Melt the butter in a saucepan, add the shallots and cook over low heat for 3 minutes, until soft. Add the white wine, cream and saffron infusion. Bring to a boil, reduce the heat and simmer gently for 5 minutes, or until the sauce thickens to a coating consistency. Add the lemon zest and juice, with salt and pepper to taste.

COOK'S TIP
Frozen peas can easily be used instead of fresh peas. Add to the asparagus after 3–4 minutes and cook until tender.

2 Bring a large saucepan of lightly salted water to a boil. Blanch the asparagus tips, scoop them out and add them to the sauce, then cook the peas and short asparagus rounds in the boiling water until just tender. Scoop them out and add to the sauce.

3 Cook the somen noodles in the same water until just tender, following the directions on the package. Drain, place in a wide pan and pour the sauce over the top.

4 Toss the noodles with the sauce and vegetables, adding the chervil and more salt and pepper if needed. Finally, sprinkle with the grated Parmesan, if using, and serve hot.

Fried Noodles with Bean Sprouts and Baby Asparagus

This dish is simplicity itself, with a wonderful contrast of textures and flavors. Use young asparagus, which is beautifully tender and cooks in minutes.

Serves 2

INGREDIENTS

4 ounces dried thin or medium egg
  noodles
4 tablespoons oil
1 small onion, chopped
1-inch piece fresh ginger root, grated
2 garlic cloves, crushed
6 ounces young asparagus, trimmed
½ cup bean sprouts
4 scallions, sliced
3 tablespoons light soy sauce
salt and freshly ground black pepper

egg noodles   *onion*

garlic

fresh ginger root   *bean sprouts*

asparagus   *scallions*   *light soy sauce*

1 Bring a pan of salted water to a boil. Add the noodles and cook for 2–3 minutes, until just tender. Drain and toss in 2 tablespoons of the oil.

2 Heat the remaining oil in a wok or frying pan until very hot. Add the onion, ginger and garlic and stir-fry for 2–3 minutes. Add the asparagus and stir-fry for another 2–3 minutes.

3 Add the noodles and bean sprouts and stir-fry for 2 minutes.

4 Stir in the scallions and soy sauce. Season to taste, adding salt sparingly, because the soy sauce will add quite a salty flavor. Stir-fry for 1 minute and serve at once.

Vegetable Chow Mein with Cashew Nuts

Chow mein is a popular dish that can be served with almost any type of Chinese vegetarian, meat or fish dish.

Serves 3–4

INGREDIENTS

2 tablespoons oil
½ cup cashew nuts
2 carrots, cut into thin strips
3 celery ribs, cut into thin strips
1 green bell pepper, seeded and cut into thin strips
1 cup bean sprouts
8 ounces dried medium or thin egg noodles
2 tablespoons toasted sesame seeds, to garnish

FOR THE LEMON SAUCE

2 tablespoons light soy sauce
1 tablespoon dry sherry
⅔ cup vegetable stock
2 lemons
1 tablespoon sugar
2 teaspoons cornstarch

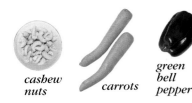
cashew nuts   *carrots*   *green bell pepper*

bean sprouts   *dried egg noodles*

toasted sesame seeds   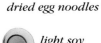 *light soy sauce*   *lemon*

1 Stir all the ingredients for the lemon sauce together in a measuring cup. Bring a large saucepan of salted water to a boil.

2 Heat the oil in a wok or large, heavy frying pan. Add the cashew nuts, toss quickly over high heat until golden, then remove with a slotted spoon.

3 Add the carrots and celery to the pan and stir-fry for 4–5 minutes. Add the pepper and bean sprouts and stir-fry for 2–3 minutes more. At the same time, cook the noodles in the pan of boiling water for 3 minutes, or according to the instructions on the package. Drain well and place in a warmed serving dish.

4 Remove the vegetables from the pan with a slotted spoon. Pour in the lemon sauce and cook for 2 minutes, stirring until thick. Return the vegetables to the pan, add the cashew nuts and stir quickly to coat in the sauce.

5 Spoon the vegetables and sauce over the noodles. Sprinkle with sesame seeds and serve.

Rice Noodles with Beef and Chili Bean Sauce

This is an excellent combination—tender beef with a chili bean sauce tossed with silky-smooth rice noodles.

Serves 4

INGREDIENTS
1 pound fresh rice noodles
¼ cup oil
1 onion, finely sliced
2 garlic cloves, finely chopped
2 slices fresh ginger root, finely chopped
8 ounces mixed bell peppers, seeded and sliced
12 ounces sirloin steak, finely sliced against the grain
3 tablespoons fermented black beans, rinsed in warm water, drained and chopped
2 tablespoons dark soy sauce
2 tablespoons oyster sauce
1 tablespoon chili bean sauce
1 tablespoon cornstarch
½ cup beef stock or water
2 scallions, finely chopped, and 2 red chiles, seeded and finely sliced, to garnish

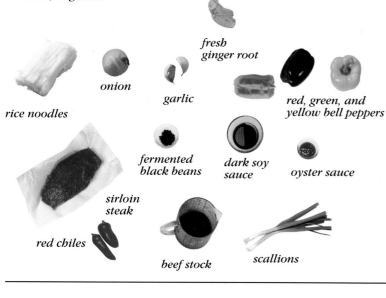

rice noodles

onion

garlic

fresh ginger root

red, green, and yellow bell peppers

fermented black beans

dark soy sauce

oyster sauce

sirloin steak

red chiles

beef stock

scallions

1 Rinse the noodles under hot water and drain well. Heat half the oil in a wok or frying pan, swirling it around. Add the onion, garlic, ginger and pepper slices.

2 Stir-fry for 3–5 minutes, then remove and keep warm. Add the remaining oil to the wok and swirl to coat the pan. When hot, add the sliced beef and fermented black beans and stir-fry over high heat for 5 minutes, or until they are cooked.

3 In a small bowl, blend the soy sauce, oyster sauce and chili bean sauce with the cornstarch and stock or water and stir until smooth. Add the mixture to the wok, together with the onion and peppers, and cook, stirring, for 1 minute.

4 Add the noodles and mix lightly. Stir over medium heat until the noodles are heated through. Adjust the seasoning if necessary. Serve at once, garnished with the chopped scallions and finely sliced chiles.

Pork Chow Mein

Chow mein is a Cantonese speciality in which noodles are fried—either by themselves or, as here, with meat and vegetables.

Serves 2–3

INGREDIENTS

6 ounces medium egg noodles
12 ounces pork tenderloin
2 tablespoons sunflower oil
1 tablespoon sesame oil
2 garlic cloves, crushed
8 scallions, sliced
1 red bell pepper, seeded and
    roughly chopped
1 green bell pepper, seeded and
    roughly chopped
2 tablespoons dark soy sauce
3 tablespoons dry sherry
¾ cup bean sprouts
3 tablespoons chopped fresh
    flat-leaf parsley
1 tablespoon toasted sesame seeds

pork tenderloin

egg noodles

garlic

sesame oil

scallions

red bell pepper

green bell pepper

dark soy sauce

dry sherry

bean sprouts

flat-leaf parsley

toasted sesame seeds

1 Soak the noodles according to the package instructions. Drain well.

2 Thinly slice the pork tenderloin. Heat the sunflower oil in a wok or large frying pan and cook the pork over high heat, until golden brown and cooked through.

3 Add the sesame oil to the pan, with the garlic, scallions and peppers. Cook over high heat for 3–4 minutes, or until the vegetables begin to soften.

4 Reduce the heat slightly and stir in the noodles, with the soy sauce and sherry. Stir-fry for 2 minutes. Add the bean sprouts and cook for another 1–2 minutes. Stir in the parsley and serve sprinkled with the sesame seeds.

Singapore Noodles

A delicious supper dish with a stunning mix of flavors and textures.

Serves 3–4

INGREDIENTS

8 ounces dried egg noodles
3 tablespoons peanut oil
1 onion, chopped
1-inch piece fresh ginger root, finely chopped
1 garlic clove, finely chopped
1 tablespoon Madras curry powder
½ teaspoon salt
4 ounces cooked chicken or pork, finely shredded
4 ounces cooked peeled shrimp
4 ounces Chinese cabbage leaves, shredded (about 2 cups)
½ cup bean sprouts
¼ cup chicken stock
1–2 tablespoons dark soy sauce
1–2 red chiles, seeded and finely shredded
4 scallions, thinly sliced

dried egg noodles

onion

fresh ginger root

garlic

curry powder

chicken

shrimp

Chinese cabbage

bean sprouts

chicken stock

dark soy sauce

red chiles

scallions

1 Cook the noodles according to the package instructions. Rinse thoroughly under cold water and drain well. Toss in 1 tablespoon of the oil and set aside.

2 Heat a wok until hot, add the remaining oil and swirl it around. Add the onion, ginger and garlic and stir-fry for about 2 minutes.

COOK'S TIP

If possible, use peanut oil for this dish or, alternatively, toss the noodles in sesame oil.

3 Add the curry powder and salt, stir-fry for 30 seconds, then add the egg noodles, chicken or pork and shrimp. Stir-fry for 3–4 minutes.

4 Add the cabbage and bean sprouts and stir-fry for 1–2 minutes. Stir in the stock and soy sauce to taste and toss well until evenly mixed. Serve at once, sprinkled with the shredded red chiles and sliced scallions.

Thai Fried Noodles

A staple of day-to-day Thai life, this dish is often served from the food stalls that line many Thai streets.

Serves 4

INGREDIENTS

6 ounces ribbon rice noodles
2 tablespoons oil
2 garlic cloves, crushed
4 ounces pork tenderloin, finely
   chopped
2 canned anchovy fillets, chopped
2 tablespoons lemon juice
3 tablespoons fish sauce
1 tablespoon sugar
8 ounces bean curd, cubed
2 eggs, beaten
3 ounces cooked peeled shrimp
½ cup bean sprouts
½ cup unsalted roasted peanuts
5 tablespoons chopped cilantro
cilantro sprigs, to garnish (optional)
crushed red pepper and fish sauce,
   to serve

garlic

ribbon rice noodles

pork tenderloin

lemon juice

fish sauce

anchovy fillets

bean curd

eggs

sugar

cilantro

shrimp

bean sprouts

peanuts

crushed red pepper

1 Soak the noodles in boiling water according to the package instructions; drain well.

2 Heat the oil in a wok or large frying pan and cook the garlic until golden. Add the pork and stir-fry until cooked through and golden.

3 Reduce the heat slightly and stir in the anchovies, lemon juice, fish sauce and sugar. Bring to a gentle simmer.

4 Stir in the bean curd, taking care not to break it up. Fold in the noodles gently, until they are coated in the liquid.

5 Make a gap at the side of the pan and add the beaten eggs. Allow them to scramble slightly and then stir them into the noodles.

6 Stir in the shrimp and most of the bean sprouts, peanuts and cilantro. Cook until piping hot. Serve the noodles topped with the remaining bean sprouts, peanuts and chopped cilantro, sprinkled with crushed red pepper and more fish sauce, to taste. Garnish with fresh cilantro sprigs, if you like.

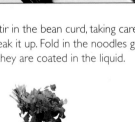

Five-Flavor Noodles

The Japanese name for this dish is *gomoku yakisoba*, meaning five different ingredients: noodles, pork, cabbage, bean sprouts and peppers.

Serves 4

INGREDIENTS

11 ounces dried Chinese thin egg
   noodles or 1¼ pound fresh
   yakisoba noodles
7 ounces pork tenderloin, thinly sliced
1½ tablespoons oil
½-inch piece fresh ginger root, grated
1 garlic clove, crushed
1¾ cups roughly chopped green
   cabbage
½ cup bean sprouts
1 green bell pepper, seeded and cut
   into fine strips
1 red bell pepper, seeded and cut
   into fine strips
salt and freshly ground black pepper
4 teaspoons ao-nori seaweed, to
   garnish (optional)

FOR THE SEASONING

4 tablespoons Worcestershire sauce
1 tablespoon light soy sauce
1 tablespoon oyster sauce
1 tablespoon sugar
white pepper

thin egg noodles

fresh ginger root

pork tenderloin

bean sprouts

garlic

green and red bell peppers

light soy sauce

1 Boil the egg noodles according to the package instructions and drain. Using a sharp chopping knife, carefully cut the pork tenderloin into 1¼–1½-inch strips and season with plenty of salt and pepper. Next, heat 1½ teaspoons of the oil in a large frying pan or wok, stir-fry the pork until just cooked, then transfer to a dish.

2 Wipe the pan with paper towels and heat the remaining oil. Add the ginger, garlic and cabbage and stir-fry for 1 minute.

3 Add the bean sprouts and stir until softened, then add the peppers and stir-fry for 1 minute.

4 Return the pork to the pan and add the noodles. Stir in all the seasoning ingredients together with a little white pepper. Stir-fry for 2–3 minutes. Sprinkle with the ao-nori seaweed, if using.

Indonesian Zucchini with Noodles

Zucchini or any other summer squash can be used in this quick and refreshing Indonesian dish, called *oseng oseng*.

Serves 4–6

INGREDIENTS
1 pound zucchini, sliced
1 onion, finely sliced
1 garlic clove, finely chopped
2 tablespoons sunflower oil
½ teaspoon ground turmeric
2 tomatoes, chopped
3 tablespoons water
4 ounces cooked, peeled shrimp, (optional)
1 ounce cellophane noodles
salt

zucchini

ground turmeric

tomatoes

shrimp

cellophane noodles

onion

garlic

1 Use a potato peeler to cut thin strips from the outside of each zucchini. Cut them into neat slices. Set the zucchini aside.

2 Sauté the onion and garlic in hot oil; do not allow them to brown. Add the turmeric, zucchini slices, chopped tomatoes, water and shrimp, if using.

3 Put the noodles in a pan and pour boiling water over to cover; set aside for a minute and then drain. Cut the noodles into 2-inch lengths and add to the vegetables.

4 Cover with a lid and allow the noodles to cook in their own steam for 2–3 minutes. Gently toss everything together well. Season with salt to taste and serve while still hot.

COOK'S TIP
Zucchini should be firm with a glossy, healthy-looking skin. Avoid any that feel squishy or generally look limp, as they will be dry and not worth using.

163

Gingered Chicken Noodles

A blend of ginger, spices and coconut milk flavors, this delicious supper dish is made in minutes. For a real Asian touch, add a little fish sauce to taste, just before serving.

Serves 2–4

INGREDIENTS
12 ounces skinless, boneless
   chicken breasts
8 ounces zucchini
10 ounces eggplant
about 2 tablespoons oil
2-inch piece fresh ginger root,
   finely chopped
6 scallions, sliced
2 teaspoons Thai green curry paste
1⅔ cups coconut milk
2 cups chicken stock
4 ounces medium egg noodles
3 tablespoons chopped cilantro
1 tablespoon lemon juice
salt and white pepper
chopped cilantro, to garnish

chicken breasts
zucchini
fresh ginger root
scallions
Thai green curry paste
eggplant
lemon
coconut milk
chicken stock
egg noodles
cilantro

COOK'S TIP
You can use fresh or dried noodles for this dish. If using dried, you will need to soak them in hot water for a few minutes to soften, then use as directed in the recipe.

1 Cut the chicken into bite-size pieces. Halve the zucchini lengthwise and roughly chop them. Cut the eggplant into similar-size pieces.

2 Heat the oil in a large saucepan or wok and cook the chicken until golden. Remove with a slotted spoon and drain on paper towels.

3 Add a little more oil, if necessary, and cook the ginger and scallions for 3 minutes. Add the zucchini and cook for 2–3 minutes. Stir in the curry paste and cook for 1 minute. Add the coconut milk, stock, eggplant and chicken, and simmer for 10 minutes.

4 Add the noodles and cook for another 5 minutes, or until the chicken is cooked and the noodles are tender. Stir in the chopped cilantro and lemon juice and adjust the seasoning. Serve garnished with chopped cilantro.

Bamie Goreng

This fried noodle dish from Indonesia is wonderfully accommodating. To the basic recipe you can add other vegetables, such as mushrooms, tiny pieces of zucchini, broccoli, leeks or bean sprouts, if you like.

Serves 6

INGREDIENTS
1 pound dried egg noodles
1 boneless, skinless chicken breast
4 ounces pork tenderloin
4 ounces calf's liver (optional)
2 eggs, beaten
6 tablespoons oil
2 tablespoons butter
2 garlic cloves, crushed
4 ounces cooked, peeled shrimp
4 ounces spinach or bok choy
2 celery ribs, finely sliced
4 scallions, cut into strips
about ¼ cup chicken stock
dark and light soy sauce
1 onion, thinly sliced
oil, for deep-frying
salt and freshly ground black pepper
celery leaves, to garnish

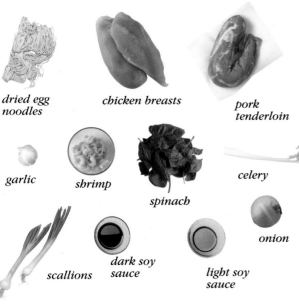

dried egg noodles

chicken breasts

pork tenderloin

garlic

shrimp

spinach

celery

scallions

dark soy sauce

light soy sauce

onion

1 Cook the noodles in salted boiling water for 3–4 minutes. Drain, rinse with cold water and drain again. Set aside until required.

2 Using a small, sharp chopping knife, finely slice the chicken breast, pork tenderloin and calf's liver, if using.

3 Season the eggs. Heat 1 teaspoon of the oil with the butter in a small pan until melted and then stir in the eggs and keep stirring until scrambled. Set aside.

4 Heat the remaining oil in a wok and fry the garlic with the chicken, pork and liver for 2–3 minutes. Add the shrimp, spinach or bok choy, celery and scallions, tossing well. Add the noodles and toss well. Add enough stock to moisten the noodles and dark and light soy sauce to taste.

5 In a separate wok or deep-fat fryer, deep-fry the onion until crisp and golden, turning constantly. Drain well. Stir the scrambled egg into the noodles and serve garnished with the fried onion and celery leaves.

Beef Noodles with Orange and Ginger

Stir-frying is one of the best ways to cook with the minimum of fat. It's also one of the quickest ways to cook, but you do need to choose tender meat.

Serves 4

INGREDIENTS

1 pound lean beef, e.g. tenderloin
    or sirloin steak, cut into
    thin strips
finely grated zest and juice of
    1 orange
1 tablespoon light soy sauce
1 teaspoon cornstarch
1-inch piece fresh ginger root,
    finely chopped
6 ounces rice noodles
2 teaspoons sesame oil
1 tablespoon sunflower oil
1 large carrot, cut into thin strips
2 scallions, thinly sliced

sirloin steak

orange

light soy sauce

fresh ginger root

carrot

sesame oil

scallions

rice noodles

1 Place the beef in a bowl and sprinkle the orange zest and juice over. If possible, set aside to marinate for at least 30 minutes.

2 Drain the liquid from the meat and set aside, then mix the meat with the soy sauce, cornstarch and ginger. Cook the noodles according to the instructions on the package. Drain well, toss with the sesame oil and keep warm.

3 Heat the sunflower oil in a wok or large frying pan and add the beef. Stir-fry for 1 minute, until lightly colored, then add the carrot and stir-fry for another 2–3 minutes.

4 Stir in the scallions and the reserved liquid from the meat, then cook, stirring, until boiling and thickened. Serve hot with the rice noodles.

Stir-fried Sweet-and-Sour Chicken

As well as being quick, this Southeast Asian dish is decidedly tasty, and you will find yourself making it again and again.

Serves 3–4

INGREDIENTS

10 ounces dried medium egg
    noodles
2 tablespoons oil
3 scallions, chopped
1 garlic clove, crushed
1-inch piece fresh ginger root,
    grated
1 teaspoon paprika
1 teaspoon ground coriander
3 boneless chicken breasts, sliced
8 ounces sugar snap peas, trimmed
4 ounces baby corn, halved
1 cup bean sprouts
1 tablespoon cornstarch
3 tablespoons light soy sauce
3 tablespoons lemon juice
1 tablespoon sugar
3 tablespoons chopped cilantro,
    to garnish

egg noodles

garlic
scallions

*ground
coriander*

chicken breasts

bean sprouts

cilantro

1 Bring a large saucepan of salted water to a boil. Add the noodles and cook according to the package instructions. Drain thoroughly, cover and keep warm.

2 Heat the oil. Add the scallions and cook over gentle heat. Mix in the next five ingredients, then stir-fry for 3–4 minutes. Add the next three ingredients and cook briefly. Add the noodles.

3 Combine the cornstarch, soy sauce, lemon juice and sugar in a small bowl. Add to the wok and simmer briefly to thicken. Serve garnished with chopped cilantro.

COOK'S TIP

Large wok lids are cumbersome and can be difficult to store in a small kitchen. Consider placing a circle of waxed paper against the food surface to keep cooking juices in.

Cellophane Noodles with Pork

Cellophane noodles absorb four times their weight in liquid and have the ability of taking on the flavor of the ingredients they are cooked with.

Serves 3–4

INGREDIENTS

4 ounces cellophane noodles
4 dried Chinese black mushrooms
8 ounces pork tenderloin
2 tablespoons dark soy sauce
2 tablespoons Chinese rice wine
2 garlic cloves, crushed
1 tablespoon grated fresh ginger root
1 teaspoon chili oil
3 tablespoons oil
4–6 scallions, chopped
1 teaspoon cornstarch blended with ¾ cup chicken stock or water
2 tablespoons chopped cilantro
salt and freshly ground black pepper
cilantro sprigs, to garnish

cellophane noodles

Chinese mushrooms

pork tenderloin

dark soy sauce

garlic

cilantro

scallions

chicken stock

fresh ginger root

1 Put the noodles and mushrooms in separate bowls and cover them with warm water. Let soak for 15–20 minutes, until soft; drain well. Cut the noodles into 5-inch lengths. Squeeze any water from the mushrooms, discard the stems and finely chop the caps.

2 Cut the pork into very small cubes. Put into a bowl with the soy sauce, rice wine, garlic, ginger and chili oil, then set aside for about 15 minutes. Drain, reserving the marinade.

3 Heat the oil in a wok and add the pork and mushrooms. Stir-fry for 3 minutes. Add the scallions and stir-fry for 1 minute. Stir in the chicken stock, marinade and seasoning.

4 Add the noodles and stir-fry for about 2 minutes, until the noodles absorb most of the liquid and the pork is cooked through. Stir in the cilantro. Serve garnished with cilantro sprigs.

Noodles with Ginger and Cilantro

Here is a simple noodle dish that goes well with most Asian dishes. It can also be served as a snack for two or three people.

Serves 4

INGREDIENTS
handful of cilantro
8 ounces dried egg noodles
3 tablespoons oil
2-inch piece fresh ginger root, cut into fine shreds
6–8 scallions, cut into shreds
2 tablespoons light soy sauce
salt and freshly ground black pepper

cilantro

dried egg noodles

fresh ginger root

scallions

light soy sauce

COOK'S TIP

As with many Thai, Singaporean or Malaysian dishes, for best results use peanut oil. Alternatively, cook vegetables in sunflower oil, but toss noodles in sesame oil.

1 Strip the leaves from the cilantro stalks. Pile them on a chopping board and coarsely chop them using a cleaver or large, sharp knife.

2 Cook the noodles according to the package instructions. Rinse under cold water, drain well and then toss in 1 tablespoon of the oil.

3 Heat a wok until hot, add the remaining oil and swirl it around. Add the ginger and stir-fry for a few seconds, then add the noodles and scallions. Stir-fry for 3–4 minutes, until hot.

4 Sprinkle the soy sauce, cilantro and seasoning over. Toss well and serve at once.

Lemongrass Shrimp on Crisp Noodle Cake

For an elegant meal, make four individual noodle cakes instead of one.

Serves 4

INGREDIENTS

11 ounces thin egg noodles
¼ cup oil
1¼ pounds medium raw king
    shrimp, peeled and deveined
½ teaspoon ground coriander
1 tablespoon ground turmeric
2 garlic cloves, finely chopped
2 slices fresh ginger root, finely
    chopped
2 lemongrass stalks, finely chopped
2 shallots, finely chopped
1 tablespoon tomato paste
1 cup coconut cream
1–2 tablespoons fresh lime juice
1–2 tablespoons fish sauce
4–6 kaffir lime leaves (optional)
1 cucumber, peeled, seeded and cut
    into 2-inch sticks
1 tomato, seeded and cut into strips
2 red chiles, seeded and finely sliced
salt and freshly ground black pepper
2 scallions, cut into thin strips, and
    a few cilantro sprigs, to garnish

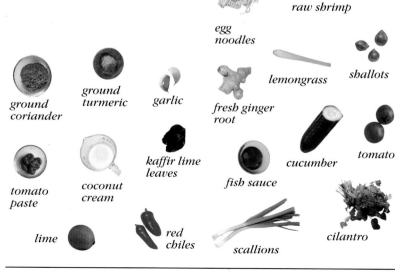

raw shrimp

egg noodles

lemongrass

shallots

ground coriander

ground turmeric

garlic

fresh ginger root

kaffir lime leaves

fish sauce

cucumber

tomato

tomato paste

coconut cream

lime

red chiles

scallions

cilantro

COOK'S TIP
Coconut cream is available in cans at supermarkets and Asian stores. It is richer than coconut milk, but this can be used if coconut cream is unavailable.

1 Cook the egg noodles in a saucepan of boiling water until just tender. Drain, rinse under cold running water and drain well.

2 Heat 1 tablespoon of the oil in a large frying pan. Add the noodles, distributing them evenly, and fry for 4–5 minutes, until crisp and golden. Turn the noodle cake over and fry the other side. Alternatively, make four individual cakes. Keep warm.

4 Stir the tomato paste and coconut cream into the juices in the pan. Stir in lime juice to taste and season with the fish sauce. Bring the sauce to a simmer, add the shrimp, then add the kaffir lime leaves, if using, and the cucumber. Simmer until the shrimp are cooked.

3 In a bowl, toss the shrimp with the ground coriander, turmeric, garlic, ginger and lemongrass. Season to taste. Heat the remaining oil in a frying pan. Add the shallots, cook for 1 minute, then add the shrimp and cook for 2 minutes more before removing with a slotted spoon.

5 Add the tomato, stir until just warmed through, then add the chiles. Serve on top of the crisp noodle cake(s), garnished with strips of scallions and cilantro sprigs.

Japanese Sweet Soy Salmon with Noodles

Teriyaki sauce forms the marinade for the salmon in this recipe. Served with soft-fried noodles, it makes a stunning dish.

Serves 3–4

INGREDIENTS
12 ounces salmon fillet
2 tablespoons Japanese soy sauce (shoyu)
2 tablespoons sake
4 tablespoons mirin or sweet sherry
1 teaspoon light brown sugar
2 teaspoons grated fresh ginger root
3 garlic cloves, 1 crushed and 2 sliced into rounds
2 tablespoons peanut oil
8 ounces dried egg noodles, cooked and drained
2 ounces alfalfa sprouts
2 tablespoons sesame seeds, lightly toasted

salmon

Japanese soy sauce

sake

garlic

mirin

fresh ginger root

noodles

peanut oil

alfalfa sprouts

sesame seeds

COOK'S TIP

It is important to scrape the marinade off the fish, because any remaining pieces of ginger or garlic will burn and spoil the finished dish.

1 Using a sharp chopping knife, cut the salmon into thin slices, then place in a shallow dish.

2 In a bowl, mix together the soy sauce, sake, mirin or sherry, brown sugar, ginger and crushed garlic. Pour over the salmon, cover and let sit for 30 minutes.

3 Preheat the broiler. Drain the salmon, scraping off and reserving the marinade. Place the salmon in a single layer on a baking sheet. Broil for 2–3 minutes without turning.

4 Meanwhile, heat a wok until hot, add the oil and swirl it around. Add the garlic rounds and cook until golden brown but not burned.

5 Add the cooked noodles and reserved marinade to the wok and stir-fry for 3–4 minutes, until the marinade has reduced slightly to a syrupy glaze and coats the noodles.

6 Toss in the alfalfa sprouts, then remove immediately from the heat. Transfer to warmed serving plates and top with the salmon. Sprinkle with the toasted sesame seeds. Serve at once.

Celebration Thai Noodles

This Thai speciality, called *mee krob*, is a crisp tangle of fried rice vermicelli tossed in a piquant sauce. It is served at weddings and other special occasions.

Serves 4

INGREDIENTS
oil, for deep-frying
6 ounces rice vermicelli
1 tablespoon chopped garlic
4–6 dried chiles, seeded and chopped
2 tablespoons chopped shallot
1 tablespoon dried shrimp, rinsed
4 ounces ground pork
4 ounces uncooked, peeled shrimp, chopped
2 tablespoons brown bean sauce
2 tablespoons rice wine vinegar
3 tablespoons fish sauce
3 tablespoons palm sugar or brown sugar
2 tablespoons tamarind or lime juice
½ cup bean sprouts

FOR THE GARNISH
2 scallions, cut into thin strips
cilantro leaves
2-egg omelet, rolled and sliced
2 red chiles, seeded and chopped
2 heads pickled garlic (optional)

rice vermicelli noodles   *garlic*   *chiles*   *dried shrimp*   *ground pork*   *uncooked shrimp*   *bean sprouts*   *scallions*

1 Heat the oil in a wok. Break the rice vermicelli apart into small handfuls about 3 inches long. Deep-fry in the hot oil until they puff up. Remove and drain on paper towels.

2 Carefully pour off all but 2 tablespoons of the hot oil from the wok. Add the garlic, chiles, shallots and dried shrimp. Cook until fragrant, then add the ground pork and stir-fry for 3–4 minutes, until it is no longer pink. Add the shrimp and stir-fry for another 2 minutes. Transfer the mixture to a plate and set aside.

3 Stir the brown bean sauce, vinegar, fish sauce and palm or brown sugar into the wok. Bring to a gentle boil, stir to dissolve the sugar and cook until thick and syrupy. Add the tamarind or lime juice and adjust the seasoning. It should be sweet, sour and salty.

4 Reduce the heat. Add the pork and shrimp mixture and the bean sprouts to the sauce, stir to mix and then add the rice noodles, tossing gently to coat them with the sauce. Transfer the noodles to a platter. Garnish with scallions, cilantro leaves, omelet strips, red chiles and pickled garlic, if you like.

Shrimp Thai Noodles

This delicately flavored dish is considered one of the national dishes of Thailand, where it is known as *pad thai*.

Serves 4–6

INGREDIENTS

12 ounces rice noodles
3 tablespoons oil
1 tablespoon chopped garlic
16 uncooked shrimp, peeled, tails
   left intact and deveined
2 eggs, lightly beaten
1 tablespoon dried shrimp, rinsed
2 tablespoons pickled daikon
   (Chinese radish)
2 ounces fried bean curd, cut into
   small slivers
½ teaspoon crushed red peppers
4 ounces Chinese chives, cut into
   2-inch lengths
1 cup bean sprouts
2 ounces roasted peanuts, coarsely
   ground
1 teaspoon sugar
1 tablespoon dark soy sauce
2 tablespoons fish sauce
2 tablespoons tamarind or lime juice
cilantro leaves, to garnish
lime wedges, to serve (optional)

rice noodles *garlic* *shrimp* *eggs* *dried shrimp* *fried bean curd* *bean sprouts* *dark soy sauce* *Chinese chives* *fish sauce* *cilantro*

1 Soak the noodles in warm water for 20–30 minutes, then drain. Heat 1 tablespoon of the oil in a wok or large frying pan. Add the garlic and cook until golden. Stir in the shrimp and cook for 1–2 minutes, until pink, tossing from time to time. Transfer to a plate.

2 Heat another 1 tablespoon of oil in the wok. Add the eggs, tilting the wok to spread them into a thin sheet. Scramble and then transfer to a plate and set aside. Heat the remaining oil and add the dried shrimp, pickled daikon, bean curd and crushed red peppers. Stir briefly.

3 Add the noodles and stir-fry for 5 minutes, then add the Chinese chives, half the bean sprouts and half the peanuts. Season with the sugar, soy sauce, fish sauce and tamarind or lime juice. Mix well.

4 When the noodles are cooked through, return the shrimp and cooked eggs to the wok and mix together. Serve garnished with the rest of the bean sprouts, peanuts and the cilantro leaves, with lime wedges if you wish.

Beef and Vegetables in Tabletop Broth

The perfect introduction to Japanese cooking, this dish is well suited to festive gatherings.

Serves 4–6

INGREDIENTS

1 pound beef sirloin, trimmed
7½ cups kombu and bonito stock, or ½ envelope instant dashi powder or ½ vegetable bouillon cube with 7½ cups water
5 ounces carrots
6 scallions, trimmed and sliced
5 ounces bok choy, roughly shredded (about 2½ cups)
8 ounces daikon (Chinese radish), peeled and shredded
10 ounces udon or fine wheat noodles, cooked
4 ounces canned bamboo shoots, sliced
6 ounces bean curd, cut into large dice
10 shiitake mushrooms

FOR THE SESAME DIPPING SAUCE

2 ounces sesame seeds or 2 tablespoons tahini paste
½ cup instant dashi stock or vegetable stock
¼ cup dark soy sauce
2 teaspoons sugar
2 tablespoons sake (optional)
2 teaspoons wasabi powder (optional)

FOR THE PONZU DIPPING SAUCE

5 tablespoons lemon juice
1 tablespoon rice wine or white wine vinegar
5 tablespoons dark soy sauce
1 tablespoon tamari sauce
1 tablespoon mirin or 1 teaspoon sugar
¼ teaspoon instant dashi powder or ¼ vegetable bouillon cube

beef

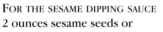
kombu and bonito stock

carrots

scallions

bok choy

udon noodles

bamboo shoots

bean curd

shiitake mushrooms

sesame seeds

dark soy sauce

sake

lemon juice

mirin

1 Slice the meat thinly with a large knife or cleaver. Arrange neatly on a plate, cover and set aside. In a Japanese donabe, or any other covered, flameproof casserole that is unglazed on the outside, bring the kombu and bonito stock, and dashi powder or stock cube and water to a boil. Cover and simmer for 8–10 minutes. Place at the table, standing on its own heat source.

2 To prepare the vegetables, bring a saucepan of salted water to a boil. Peel the carrots and with a zester cut a series of grooves along their length. Slice the carrots thinly and blanch for 2–3 minutes. Blanch the scallions, bok choy and daikon for the same time. Arrange the vegetables with the noodles, bamboo shoots and bean curd. Slice the mushrooms.

3 To make the sesame dipping sauce, dry-fry the sesame seeds, if using, in a heavy frying pan, taking care not to burn them. Grind the seeds smooth using a mortar and pestle with a rough surface. Alternatively, you can use tahini paste. Add the remaining sesame dipping sauce ingredients, combine well, then pour into a shallow dish.

4 To make the ponzu dipping sauce, put the ingredients into a screw-top jar and shake well. Provide your guests with chopsticks and individual bowls, so they can help themselves to what they want. The idea is to cook their choice of meat and vegetables in the stock and flavor these with either the sesame or ponzu dipping sauce. Toward the end of the meal, each guest takes a portion of noodles and ladles the well-flavored stock over them.

Clay Pot of Chili Squid and Noodles

This dish is delicious in its own right, or served as part of a larger Chinese meal, with other meat or fish dishes and rice.

Serves 2–4

INGREDIENTS

1½–1 pound fresh squid
2 tablespoons oil
3 slices fresh ginger root,
    finely chopped
2 garlic cloves, finely chopped
1 red onion, finely sliced
1 carrot, finely sliced
1 celery rib, sliced
    diagonally
2 ounces sugar snap peas, trimmed
pinch of salt
1 teaspoon sugar
1 tablespoon chili bean paste
½ teaspoon chili powder
3 ounces cellophane noodles,
    soaked in hot water until soft
½ cup chicken stock or water
1 tablespoon light soy sauce
1 tablespoon oyster sauce
1 teaspoon sesame oil
cilantro leaves, to garnish

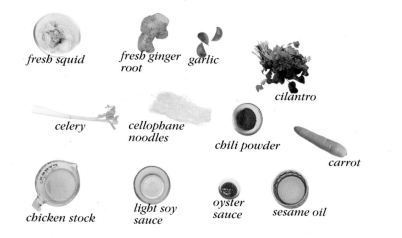

fresh squid *fresh ginger root* *garlic* *cilantro* *celery* *cellophane noodles* *chili powder* *carrot* *chicken stock* *light soy sauce* *oyster sauce* *sesame oil*

1 Prepare the squid. Holding the body in one hand, gently pull away the head and tentacles. Discard the head; trim and reserve the tentacles. Remove the "quill" from inside the body of the squid. Peel off the brown skin on the outside. Rub salt into the squid and wash under water. Cut the body of the squid into rings or split it open lengthwise, score crisscross patterns on the inside of the body and cut it into 2 x 1½-inch pieces.

2 Heat the oil in a large, flameproof casserole or wok. Add the ginger, garlic and onion and cook for 1–2 minutes. Add the squid, carrot, celery and sugar snap peas. Cook until the squid curls up. Season with salt and sugar and then stir in the chili bean paste and chili powder. Transfer the mixture to a bowl and set aside until required. Drain the soaked noodles and add to the casserole or wok.

3 Stir in the chicken stock or water, light soy sauce and oyster sauce. Cover and cook over medium heat for 10 minutes, or until the noodles are tender. Return the squid and vegetable mixture to the pot.

4 Cover and cook for another 5–6 minutes, until all the flavors are combined. Season to taste.

5 Spoon the mixture into a warmed clay pot and drizzle with the sesame oil. Sprinkle with the cilantro leaves and serve immediately.

COOK'S TIP
These noodles have a smooth, light texture that readily absorbs the other flavors in the dish. To vary the flavor, the vegetables can be altered according to what is available.

Tiger Shrimp and Lap Cheong Noodles

Lap cheong is a special air-dried Chinese sausage. It is available at most Chinese markets. If you cannot buy it, substitute with diced ham, chorizo or salami.

Serves 4–6

INGREDIENTS

3 tablespoons oil
2 garlic cloves, sliced
1 teaspoon chopped fresh ginger
    root
2 red chiles, seeded and chopped
2 lap cheong, about 3 ounces,
    rinsed and sliced
1 boneless chicken breast, thinly
    sliced
16 uncooked tiger shrimp, peeled,
    tails left intact and deveined
4 ounces green beans
1 cup bean sprouts
2 ounces Chinese chives
1 pound egg noodles, cooked in
    boiling water until tender
2 tablespoons dark soy sauce
1 tablespoon oyster sauce
salt and freshly ground black pepper
1 tablespoon sesame oil
2 scallions, cut into strips, and
    cilantro leaves, to garnish

red chiles

chicken breast

shrimp

garlic

green beans

bean sprouts

Chinese chives

egg noodles

dark soy sauce

fresh ginger root

oyster sauce

sesame oil

scallions

cilantro

COOK'S TIP

Chinese chives, sometimes called garlic chives, have a delicate garlic/onion flavor. If they are not available, use the green parts of scallions.

1 Heat 1 tablespoon of the oil in a wok or large frying pan and sauté the garlic, ginger and chiles.

2 Add the lap cheong, chicken, shrimp and beans. Stir-fry over high heat for about 2 minutes, or until the chicken and shrimp are cooked. Transfer the mixture to a bowl and set aside.

3 Heat the remaining oil in the wok and add the bean sprouts and Chinese chives. Stir-fry for 1–2 minutes.

4 Add the noodles and toss and stir to mix. Season with soy sauce, oyster sauce, salt and pepper.

5 Return the shrimp mixture to the wok. Reheat and mix well with the noodles. Stir in the sesame oil. Serve garnished with scallions and cilantro leaves.

Deluxe Fried Noodles

This makes a tasty side dish for three to four people or a meal for two people, served with just a separate vegetable or meat dish.

Serves 2–4

INGREDIENTS
1½ ounces dried Chinese mushrooms
10 ounces fine egg noodles
1 tablespoon sesame oil
3 tablespoons oil
2 garlic cloves, crushed
1 onion, chopped
2 green chiles, seeded and thinly sliced
1 tablespoon curry powder
6 ounces green beans
4 ounces bok choy, thinly shredded (about 2 cups)
6 scallions, sliced
3 tablespoons dark soy sauce
6 ounces cooked, peeled shrimp
salt

Chinese mushrooms

egg noodles

sesame oil   *garlic*   *onion*

green chiles   *curry powder*

green beans   *bok choy*

shrimp   *dark soy sauce*   *scallions*

1 Place the mushrooms in a bowl. Cover with warm water and soak for 30 minutes. Drain, reserving 3 tablespoons of the soaking water, then slice, discarding the stems.

2 Cook the noodles in a pan of lightly salted boiling water according to the directions on the package. Drain, place in a bowl and toss with the sesame oil.

3 Heat a wok, add the oil and stir-fry the garlic, onion and chiles for 3 minutes. Stir in the curry powder and cook for 1 minute, then add the mushrooms, beans, bok choy and scallions. Stir-fry for 3–4 minutes.

4 Add the noodles, soy sauce, reserved mushroom soaking water and shrimp. Toss over the heat for 2–3 minutes, until the noodles and shrimp are heated through, then serve.

Chicken Curry with Rice Vermicelli

Lemongrass gives this Southeast Asian curry a wonderful, lemony flavor and fragrance.

Serves 4

INGREDIENTS
1 chicken, 3–3½ pounds
8 ounces sweet potatoes
¼ cup oil
1 onion, finely sliced
3 garlic cloves, crushed
2–3 tablespoons Thai curry powder
salt
1 teaspoon sugar
2 teaspoons fish sauce
2½ cups coconut milk
1 lemongrass stalk, cut in half
12 ounces rice vermicelli, soaked in
    hot water until soft

FOR THE GARNISH
½ cup bean sprouts
2 scallions, finely sliced diagonally
2 red chiles, seeded and finely sliced
8–10 mint leaves

chicken

Thai curry powder

coconut milk

rice vermicelli noodles

lemongrass

bean sprouts

mint leaves

red chiles

scallions

1 Skin the chicken. Cut the flesh into small pieces. Peel the sweet potatoes and cut them into large chunks, about the size of the chicken pieces.

2 Heat half the oil in a large, heavy saucepan. Add the onion and garlic and cook until the onion softens. Add the chicken pieces and stir-fry until they change color. Stir in the curry powder. Season with salt and sugar and mix thoroughly, then add the fish sauce, coconut milk and lemongrass. Cook over low heat for 15 minutes.

3 Meanwhile, heat the remaining oil in a large frying pan. Fry the sweet potatoes until lightly golden. Using a slotted spoon, add them to the chicken. Cook for 10–15 minutes more, or until both the chicken and sweet potatoes are tender.

4 Drain the rice vermicelli and cook them in a saucepan of boiling water for 3–5 minutes. Drain well. Place in shallow bowls, with the chicken curry. Garnish with bean sprouts, scallions, chiles and mint leaves, and serve.

Birthday Noodles with Hoisin Lamb

In China, the noodles served at birthday celebrations are left long: It is held that cutting them might shorten one's life.

Serves 4

INGREDIENTS
2¼ pounds lean boneless
   lamb shoulder
2 tablespoons oil
12 ounces thick egg noodles
4 ounces haricots verts (French
   green beans), blanched
salt and freshly ground black pepper
2 hard-boiled eggs, halved
2 scallions, finely shredded, to garnish

FOR THE MARINADE
2 garlic cloves, crushed
2 teaspoons grated fresh ginger root
2 tablespoons dark soy sauce
2 tablespoons rice wine
1–2 dried red chiles
2 tablespoons oil

FOR THE SAUCE
1 tablespoon cornstarch
2 tablespoons dark soy sauce
2 tablespoons rice wine
grated zest and juice of ½ orange
1 tablespoon hoisin sauce
1 tablespoon wine vinegar
1 teaspoon, light brown sugar

1 Cut the lamb into 2-inch-thick medallions. Mix the ingredients for the marinade in a large, shallow dish. Add the lamb and marinate in the refrigerator for at least 4 hours or overnight. Bring a large saucepan of water to a boil. Add the noodles and cook for 2 minutes only. Drain, rinse under cold water and drain again. Set aside.

2 Heat the oil in a heavy saucepan or flameproof casserole. Sauté the lamb for 5 minutes, until browned. Add just enough water to cover the meat. Bring to a boil, skim, then reduce the heat and simmer for 40 minutes, or until the meat is tender, adding more water as necessary.

3 Make the sauce. Blend the cornstarch with the remaining ingredients in a bowl. Stir into the lamb and mix well without breaking up the meat.

4 Add the noodles with the beans. Simmer gently until both are cooked. Add salt and pepper to taste. Divide the noodle mixture among four large bowls, garnish each portion with half a hard-boiled egg, sprinkle with scallions and serve.

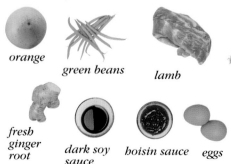

orange

green beans

lamb

scallions

garlic

fresh ginger root

dark soy sauce

hoisin sauce

eggs

wine vinegar

thick egg noodles

Chicken and Shrimp Hot Pot

Made in a portable hot pot, this dish, known as Yosenabe, combines meat, fish, vegetables and noodles to create a warming meal that is cooked at the table.

Serves 4

INGREDIENTS
14 ounces chicken thighs or breasts on the bone
8 uncooked tiger shrimp
7 ounces dried udon noodles
4 shiitake mushrooms, stems removed
½ head bok choy, cut into 1¼-in slices
3 leeks, sliced diagonally into pieces ½ in-thick
6 x 4-inch piece bean curd (about 5 ounces), cut into 1¼-inch cubes
11 ounces shirataki noodles, boiled for 2 minutes, drained and halved

FOR THE YOSENABE STOCK
4 cups kombu and bonito stock
6 tablespoons sake or dry white wine
2 tablespoons dark soy sauce
4 teaspoons mirin
2 teaspoons salt

udon noodles

shiitake mushrooms

bok choy

tiger shrimp

leeks

sake

mirin

kombu and bonito stock

bean curd

dark soy sauce

chicken thighs

1 Cut the chicken into ½-inch chunks. Remove the black intestinal vein from the shrimp if necessary.

2 Cook the udon noodles for 2 minutes less than the package instructions dictate, drain and rinse thoroughly, then drain again and set aside. Arrange all the remaining ingredients on large plates.

3 Bring all the ingredients for the yosenabe stock to a boil in the hot pot. Add the chicken and simmer for 3 minutes, skimming the broth throughout cooking.

4 Add the remaining ingredients, except the udon noodles and simmer for 5 minutes, or until cooked. Diners serve themselves from the simmering hot pot. Finally, when all the ingredients have been eaten, add the udon noodles to the rest of the soup, heat through and serve in bowls to round off the meal.

index